Achieve great Chemistry with CGP!

Let's deal with the bad news first: AQA's Foundation Level GCSE Chemistry course is pretty tough, so you'll need to be fully prepared for exam day.

Here's the good news: this fantastic CGP book is absolutely jam-packed with all the exam-style practice you'll need — it even covers all the new required practicals.

And since you'll be tested on lots of topics in the real exams, we've also included a section of mixed questions to keep you on your toes!

CGP — still the best! ☺

Our sole aim here at CGP is to produce the highest quality books — carefully written, immaculately presented and dangerously close to being funny.

Then we work our socks off to get them out to you
— at the cheapest possible prices.

Contents

✓ Use the tick boxes to check off the topics you've completed.

How to Use This Book...iv
What to Expect in the Exams......................................v

Topic 1 — Atomic Structure and the Periodic Table

Atoms.. 2
Elements... 3
Compounds... 4
Chemical Equations.. 5
Mixtures.. 6
Chromatography... 7
More Separation Techniques................................... 8
Distillation... 9
The History of The Atom.. 10
Electronic Structure.. 11
Development of The Periodic Table...................... 12
The Modern Periodic Table..................................... 13
Metals and Non-Metals.. 14
Group 1 Elements... 15
Transition Metals.. 16
Group 7 Elements... 17
Group 0 Elements... 18

Topic 2 — Bonding, Structure and Properties of Matter

Formation of Ions... 19
Ionic Bonding... 20
Ionic Compounds... 21
Covalent Bonding.. 22
Simple Molecular Substances............................... 23
Polymers and Giant Covalent Structures............. 25
Structures of Carbon.. 26
Metallic Bonding.. 27
States of Matter... 28
Changing State... 29
Nanoparticles... 30
Uses of Nanoparticles.. 31

Topic 3 — Quantitative Chemistry

Relative Formula Mass... 32
Conservation of Mass.. 33
Concentrations of Solutions.................................. 35
Atom Economy... 36
Percentage Yield.. 37

Topic 4 — Chemical Changes

Acids and Bases... 38
Titrations.. 39
Reactions of Acids... 40
The Reactivity Series and Extracting Metals....... 42
Reactions of Metals... 43
Electrolysis... 44

Topic 5 — Energy Changes

Exothermic and Endothermic Reactions.............. 46
Measuring Energy Changes................................... 47
Reaction Profiles.. 48
Cells, Batteries and Fuel Cells.............................. 49

Topic 6 — The Rate and Extent of Chemical Change

Rates of Reaction... 51
Factors Affecting Rates of Reaction...................... 52
Measuring Rates of Reaction................................. 53
More on Measuring Rates...................................... 54
Graphs of Reaction Rate Experiments.................. 55
Working Out Reaction Rates................................. 56
Reversible Reactions.. 57

Topic 7 — Organic Chemistry

Hydrocarbons... 58
Crude Oil.. 59
Fractional Distillation.. 60
Cracking... 61
Alkenes... 62
Reactions of Alkenes... 63
Addition Polymers... 65
Naturally Occurring Polymers............................... 66
Alcohols.. 67
Carboxylic Acids.. 69

Topic 8 — Chemical Analysis

Purity and Formulations 70
Paper Chromatography 71
Using Chromatograms 72
Tests for Gases 73
Tests for Ions 74
Flame Emission Spectroscopy 76

Topic 9 — Chemistry of the Atmosphere

The Evolution of the Atmosphere 77
Greenhouse Gases and Climate Change 78
Carbon Footprints 79
Air Pollution 80

Topic 10 — Using Resources

Ceramics, Polymers and Composites 81
Properties of Materials 82
Corrosion 83
Finite and Renewable Resources 84
Reuse and Recycling 85
Life Cycle Assessments 86
Using Life Cycle Assessments 87
Potable Water 88
Desalination 89
Waste Water Treatment 90
The Haber Process 91
NPK Fertilisers 92

Mixed Questions

Mixed Questions 93

Published by CGP

Editors:
Dan Chesman, Paul Jordin, Charles Kitts, Caroline Purvis

Contributors:
Ian Davis, Chris Workman

With thanks to Katherine Faudemer and Jamie Sinclair for the proofreading.

With thanks to Ana Pungartnik for the copyright research.

Graph on page 78 based on data provided by NOAA ESRL Global Monitoring Division, Boulder, Colorado, USA (http://esrl.noaa.gov/gmd/). By Dr. Pieter Tans, NOAA/ESRL (www.esrl.noaa.gov/gmd/ccgg/trends/) and Dr. Ralph Keeling, Scripps Institution of Oceanography (scrippsco2.ucsd.edu/).

ISBN: 978 1 78908 325 5

Clipart from Corel®
Printed by Elanders Ltd, Newcastle upon Tyne

Based on the classic CGP style created by Richard Parsons.

Text, design, layout and original illustrations © Coordination Group Publications Ltd. (CGP) 2019
All rights reserved.

Photocopying this book is not permitted, even if you have a CLA licence.
Extra copies are available from CGP with next day delivery • 0800 1712 712 • www.cgpbooks.co.uk

How to Use This Book

- Hold the book <u>upright</u>, approximately <u>50 cm</u> from your face, ensuring that the text looks like <u>this</u>, not this.
- In case of emergency, press the two halves of the book together <u>firmly</u> in order to close.
- Before attempting to use this book, read the following <u>safety information</u>:

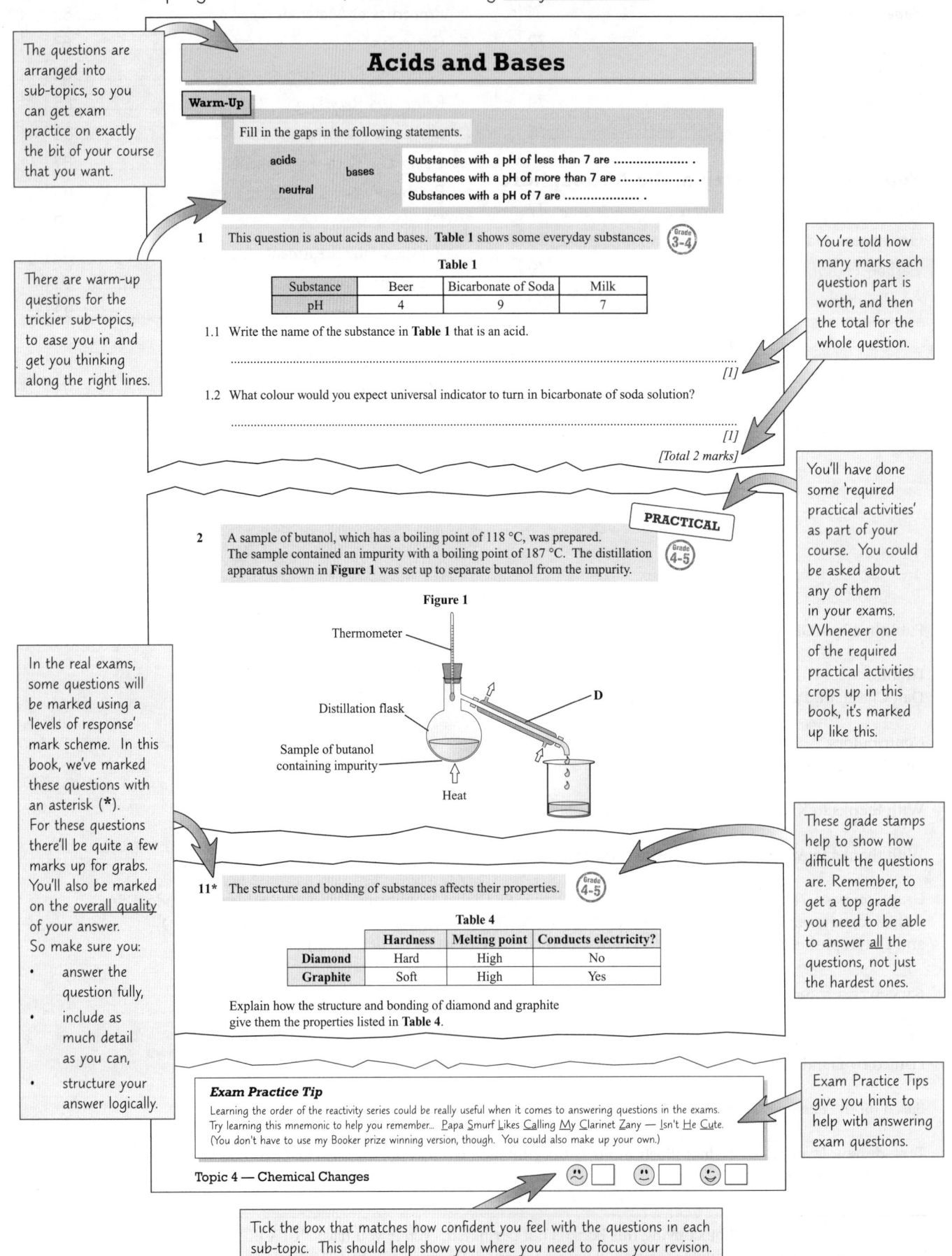

The questions are arranged into sub-topics, so you can get exam practice on exactly the bit of your course that you want.

Acids and Bases

Warm-Up

Fill in the gaps in the following statements.

acids
bases
neutral

Substances with a pH of less than 7 are ....
Substances with a pH of more than 7 are ....
Substances with a pH of 7 are ....

1   This question is about acids and bases. **Table 1** shows some everyday substances. *(Grade 3-4)*

Table 1

Substance	Beer	Bicarbonate of Soda	Milk
pH	4	9	7

1.1 Write the name of the substance in **Table 1** that is an acid.

....
[1]

1.2 What colour would you expect universal indicator to turn in bicarbonate of soda solution?

....
[1]

[Total 2 marks]

There are warm-up questions for the trickier sub-topics, to ease you in and get you thinking along the right lines.

You're told how many marks each question part is worth, and then the total for the whole question.

PRACTICAL

2   A sample of butanol, which has a boiling point of 118 °C, was prepared. The sample contained an impurity with a boiling point of 187 °C. The distillation apparatus shown in **Figure 1** was set up to separate butanol from the impurity. *(Grade 4-5)*

Figure 1

Thermometer
Distillation flask
Sample of butanol containing impurity
Heat
D

You'll have done some 'required practical activities' as part of your course. You could be asked about any of them in your exams. Whenever one of the required practical activities crops up in this book, it's marked up like this.

In the real exams, some questions will be marked using a 'levels of response' mark scheme. In this book, we've marked these questions with an asterisk (*). For these questions there'll be quite a few marks up for grabs. You'll also be marked on the <u>overall quality</u> of your answer. So make sure you:
- answer the question fully,
- include as much detail as you can,
- structure your answer logically.

11* The structure and bonding of substances affects their properties. *(Grade 4-5)*

Table 4

	Hardness	Melting point	Conducts electricity?
Diamond	Hard	High	No
Graphite	Soft	High	Yes

Explain how the structure and bonding of diamond and graphite give them the properties listed in **Table 4**.

These grade stamps help to show how difficult the questions are. Remember, to get a top grade you need to be able to answer <u>all</u> the questions, not just the hardest ones.

Exam Practice Tip

Learning the order of the reactivity series could be really useful when it comes to answering questions in the exams. Try learning this mnemonic to help you remember... <u>P</u>apa <u>S</u>murf <u>L</u>ikes <u>C</u>alling <u>M</u>y <u>C</u>larinet <u>Z</u>any — <u>I</u>sn't <u>H</u>e <u>C</u>ute. (You don't have to use my Booker prize winning version, though. You could also make up your own.)

Topic 4 — Chemical Changes   ☹ ☐   ☺ ☐   😊 ☐

Exam Practice Tips give you hints to help with answering exam questions.

Tick the box that matches how confident you feel with the questions in each sub-topic. This should help show you where you need to focus your revision.

How to Use This Book

What to Expect in the Exams

Before you get cracking on some exam practice, here's a handy guide to what you'll have to face in the exams. And I've jotted down a few 'Golden Rules', too — remember those and you'll be off to a good start on exam day.

1) Topics are Covered in Different Papers

For AQA GCSE Chemistry, you'll sit two exam papers at the end of your course.

Paper	Time	No. of marks	Topics Assessed
1	1 hr 45 mins	100	1, 2, 3, 4 and 5
2	1 hr 45 mins	100	6, 7, 8, 9 and 10

You're expected to know the basic concepts of chemistry in both papers.

2) You'll be Tested on your Maths...

At least 20% of the total marks for AQA GCSE Chemistry come from questions that use maths skills. For example, you might be asked to read or draw a graph, do a calculation using a formula or work out a percentage.

3) ...and on your Practical Skills

- AQA GCSE Chemistry contains eight required practical activities. You could be asked about any of them in the exams.
- At least 15% of the total marks will be from questions testing practical skills.
- For example, you might be asked to comment on the design of an experiment (the apparatus and methods), make predictions or interpret results.

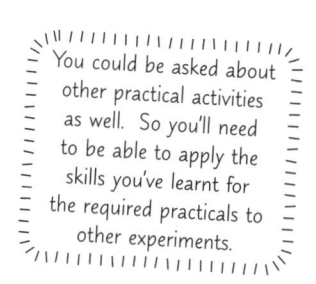

You could be asked about other practical activities as well. So you'll need to be able to apply the skills you've learnt for the required practicals to other experiments.

Seven Golden Rules for Your Exam

1) **Always, always, always make sure you read the question properly.**
   For example, if the question asks you to give your answer in cm³, don't give it in dm³.

2) **Look at the number of marks a question is worth.**
   The number of marks gives you a pretty good clue of how much to write.
   So if a question is worth four marks, make sure you write four decent points.

3) **Use specialist vocabulary.**
   You know the words I mean — the sciencey ones, like electron, covalent and oxidation. Examiners love them.

4) **Write your answers as clearly and accurately as you can.**
   For some open response questions, you'll be marked on the overall quality of your answer, as well as the scientific content. So make sure your answers have a clear and logical structure.

5) **Show each step in your calculations.**
   Even if your final answer's wrong, you could pick up some marks if the examiner can see that your method is right. Make sure you're working in the right units too — check before you put any numbers in your calculator.

6) **Pay attention to the time.**
   Don't spend ages staring at the question paper. If you're totally, hopelessly stuck on a question, just leave it and move on to the next one. You can always go back to it at the end if you've got enough time.

7) **Be prepared and try not to panic.**
   Exam day can give anyone a case of the jitters. So make sure you've got everything you need for the exam (e.g. pen, spare pen, pencil, ruler, calculator) ready the night before. Eat a good breakfast. And try to relax...

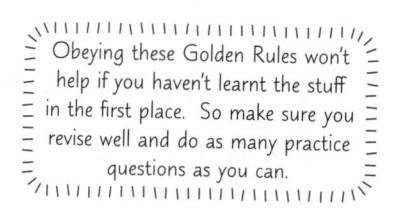

Obeying these Golden Rules won't help if you haven't learnt the stuff in the first place. So make sure you revise well and do as many practice questions as you can.

What to Expect in the Exams

Topic 1 — Atomic Structure and the Periodic Table

Atoms

Warm-Up

Choose from the words below to fill in the passage.

protons   neutrons   electrons   compounds   heavy   light

.... and .... are found in the nucleus of an atom.

.... move around the nucleus in shells.

Compared to electrons, protons and neutrons are ....

---

1 This question is about the particles inside an atom. *Grade 1-3*

1.1 Complete **Table 1**.

Table 1

Particle	Relative Charge
Proton	....
....	0
Electron	....

[3]

1.2 What is the overall charge of an atom? Tick **one** box.

Positive ☐   Negative ☐   Neutral ☐

[1]

[Total 4 marks]

---

2 A potassium atom can be represented by the nuclear symbol $^{39}_{19}K$. *Grade 4-5*

2.1 What is the mass number of a potassium atom?

....

[1]

2.2 What is the atomic number of a potassium atom?

....

[1]

2.3 How many protons, neutrons and electrons does an atom of potassium have?

protons: ....   neutrons: ....   electrons: ....

[3]

[Total 5 marks]

Topic 1 — Atomic Structure and the Periodic Table

Elements

1 Which of the following statements about elements is true?

Tick **one** box.

Atoms of the same element can contain different numbers of protons. ☐

There are about 200 different elements. ☐

Elements contain more than one type of atom. ☐

Atoms are the smallest part of an element that can exist. ☐

[Total 1 mark]

2 Bromine has two stable isotopes, A and B. **Table 1** shows some information about them.

2.1 Complete **Table 1** by calculating the number of neutrons for each isotope of bromine.

Table 1

isotope	mass number	number of protons	number of neutrons	abundance (%)
A	79	35	....	51
B	81	35	....	49

[2]

2.2 Using the information in **Table 1**, state the number of electrons in isotope A.

....
[1]

2.3 Using the information in **Table 1**, calculate the following values:

abundance of isotope A × mass number of isotope A: ....

....

abundance of isotope B × mass number of isotope B: ....

....
[2]

2.4 Calculate the relative atomic mass of bromine. Give your answer to 1 decimal place.
Use the equation:

$$\text{Relative atomic mass} = \frac{\text{sum of (isotope abundance} \times \text{isotope mass number)}}{\text{sum of abundances of all the isotopes}}$$

Relative atomic mass = ...
[2]

[Total 7 marks]

Topic 1 — Atomic Structure and the Periodic Table

Compounds

1 Ammonia is a compound with the formula NH$_3$. *(Grade 4-5)*

1.1 Why is ammonia classified as a compound? Tick **one** box.

- [ ] It contains only one type of atom.
- [ ] It contains two different elements held together by chemical bonds.
- [ ] It cannot be broken down into elements using chemical methods.
- [ ] It contains more than one atom.

[1]

1.2 How many atoms are there in a single molecule of ammonia?

....

[1]

[Total 2 marks]

2 The following list shows the chemical formulas of some different substances. *(Grade 4-5)*

A. O$_2$ **B.** NaCl   **C.** C$_2$H$_4$ **D.** H$_2$ **E.** SO$_2$Cl$_2$

2.1 Name substance **B**.

....

[1]

2.2 Identify **two** substances from the list that are compounds.

....

[2]

2.3 How many elements are there in a molecule of substance **A**?

....

[1]

2.4 State how many atoms of each element there are in one molecule of substance **E**.

S: ....

O: ....

Cl: ....

[2]

[Total 6 marks]

Exam Practice Tip

Make sure you know the difference between atoms, elements and compounds — here's a quick round up. Everything is made of atoms (which contain protons, neutrons and electrons). Elements only contain one type of atom (all the atoms have the same number of protons). A compound is made up of atoms of different elements all bonded together. Got it?

Topic 1 — Atomic Structure and the Periodic Table

Chemical Equations

Warm-Up

The word equation for a reaction is shown below:

magnesium + hydrochloric acid → magnesium chloride + hydrogen

For each of the following statements circle whether the statement is **true** or **false**.

1) Hydrogen is a product in the reaction	True Or False
2) The equation shows the reaction between chlorine and hydrogen	True Or False
3) Hydrochloric acid is a reactant	True Or False
4) The equation shows the reaction between magnesium and hydrochloric acid	True Or False

1 Look at the following word equation: calcium + water → calcium hydroxide + hydrogen

1.1 Name the **two** reactants in this reaction.

....
[1]

1.2 Name the **two** products of this reaction.

....
[1]
[Total 2 marks]

2 Sodium (Na) reacts with chlorine gas (Cl_2) to form sodium chloride (NaCl) only.

2.1 Write a word equation for this reaction.

....
[1]

2.2 Which of the following equations correctly represents this reaction?
Tick **one** box.

Na + Cl → NaCl ☐ Na_2 + 2Cl → 2NaCl ☐

Na_2 + Cl_2 → 2NaCl ☐   2Na + Cl_2 → 2NaCl ☐
[1]

2.3 Sodium also reacts with oxygen (O_2) to form sodium oxide (Na_2O).
Balance the equation for this reaction.

.... Na + O_2 → .... Na_2O
[1]
[Total 3 marks]

Topic 1 — Atomic Structure and the Periodic Table

Mixtures

1 Which of the following substances is a mixture?

Tick **one** box.

copper ☐

calcium chloride ☐

crude oil ☐

ammonia ☐

[Total 1 mark]

2 Mixtures contain different substances.

2.1 State the smallest number of substances a mixture must contain.

....
[1]

2.2 Complete the sentence that describes the different parts in a mixture.
Use words from the box.

| change | don't change | electrical | physical | chemical |

The chemical properties of the different parts in a mixture .... when

they're added together. The different parts can be separated from the mixture using

.... methods.

[2]
[Total 3 marks]

3 Air contains many gases. These gases include nitrogen, oxygen and argon.

3.1 Is air an element, a compound or a mixture? Give a reason for your answer.

Type of substance: ....

Reason: ....

....
[3]

3.2 Argon can be separated out from air. Will the chemical properties of argon as a separate gas be different from the properties of argon in air? Explain your answer.

....

....
[2]
[Total 5 marks]

Topic 1 — Atomic Structure and the Periodic Table

Chromatography

PRACTICAL

1 The first three steps for carrying out paper chromatography of an ink are shown below. *(Grade 3-4)*

1. Draw a pencil line near the bottom of a sheet of filter paper.
2. Add a spot of ink to the line.
3. Pour a small amount of solvent into a beaker.

1.1 Which of the following steps should be done next?
Tick **one** box.

Place a lid on the beaker. ☐

Place the sheet in the solvent so that the solvent is just below the pencil line. ☐

Leave the paper to dry. ☐

Let the solvent seep up the paper until it's almost reached the top. ☐

[1]

1.2 Why is pencil used to make the line on the filter paper?

....
[1]
[Total 2 marks]

2 **Figure 1** shows the result of a paper chromatography experiment to separate the dyes in an ink. *(Grade 4-5)*

Figure 1

(Diagram showing a rectangular filter paper with: Line A at the top, a spot in the middle, Dye B labelled at the bottom spot on the Pencil line.)

2.1 In **Figure 1** line A represents the point reached by the solvent. What is the name of this point?

....
[1]

2.2 Why does the ink separate into different spots of dye?

....
[1]

2.3 Dye B has stayed on the pencil line.
Predict whether Dye B is soluble or insoluble in the solvent used in the experiment.

....
[1]
[Total 3 marks]

Topic 1 — Atomic Structure and the Periodic Table

More Separation Techniques

1 Filtration is a way of separating substances.

1.1 Complete the sentence below that describes filtration.
Use the words from the box.

| soluble | insoluble | solids | liquids | solutions |

Filtration is used to separate .... solids from ....
[2]

1.2 Which two pieces of equipment would you use in a filtration experiment?
Tick **two** boxes.

Filter paper ☐   Evaporating dish ☐

Bunsen burner ☐   Funnel ☐

[2]
[Total 4 marks]

2 A mixture is made by dissolving substance **A** (a solid) in warm water.
Substance **A** breaks down at high temperatures.
Figure 1 shows the equipment that could be used to separate substance **A** from the solution.

Figure 1

Beaker   Bunsen burner   Evaporating dish   Filter paper   Funnel   Tripod, gauze and heatproof mat

2.1 Name the separation technique that you could carry out using this equipment.

....
[1]

2.2* Write a method that could be used to separate substance **A** from the water using this equipment.

....

....

....

....

....

....
[6]
[Total 7 marks]

Topic 1 — Atomic Structure and the Periodic Table

Distillation

1 A mixture contains two liquids. The liquids have similar boiling points.

Which of the following techniques would be best for separating the two liquids?
Tick **one** box.

☐ Evaporation ☐ Condensation ☐ Simple distillation ☐ Fractional distillation

[Total 1 mark]

2 A sample of butanol, which has a boiling point of 118 °C, was prepared. The sample contained an impurity with a boiling point of 187 °C. The distillation apparatus shown in **Figure 1** was set up to separate butanol from the impurity.

Figure 1

2.1 Name the piece of apparatus labelled **D**.

....
[1]

2.2 What happens to the vapour that enters the piece of apparatus labelled **D**?

....
[1]

2.3 Describe how you could use the thermometer to identify when butanol is being distilled from the mixture.

....
[1]

2.4 Suggest why butanol can't be distilled by heating the flask with a water bath.

....
....
[2]

[Total 5 marks]

Topic 1 — Atomic Structure and the Periodic Table

The History of The Atom

Warm-Up

Use the words to label the different parts of the atom shown below.

shell   electron   nucleus

....

1   Models of the atom have changed over time.

1.1 Which of the following is the best description of what scientists thought an atom was like before the electron was discovered?
Tick **one** box.

Tiny solid spheres ☐   Formless 'clouds' ☐   Flat shapes ☐   Packets of energy ☐

[1]

1.2 Number the models of the atom below in the order they were created. Put a 1 next to the first model created, a 2 next to the second model created and a 3 next to the most recent model.

Nuclear model ☐   Bohr's nuclear model ☐   Plum pudding model ☐

[2]

[Total 3 marks]

2   Scientists' understanding of the atom has changed as different particles have been discovered.

2.1 Draw **one** line from each atomic model to the correct description of that model.

Atomic Model	Description
Plum pudding model	A positively charged 'ball' with negatively charged electrons in it.
	A small positively charged nucleus surrounded by a 'cloud' of negative electrons.
Bohr's nuclear model	Electrons in fixed orbits surrounding a small positively charged nucleus.
Nuclear model	Solid spheres with a different sphere for each element.

[3]

2.2 James Chadwick discovered a neutral particle inside the nucleus. Give the name of this particle.

....

[1]

[Total 4 marks]

Topic 1 — Atomic Structure and the Periodic Table

Electronic Structure

1 Complete **Table 1** to show how many electrons go in each of the first three electron shells.

Table 1

Electron shell	Number of electrons it can hold
1st	....
2nd	....
3rd	....

[Total 3 marks]

2 Calcium has an atomic number of 20.

2.1 What is the electron configuration of a calcium atom? Tick **one** box.

☐ 2, 18   ☐ 2, 16, 2   ☐ 2, 8, 8, 2   ☐ 2, 2, 8, 8

[1]

2.2 Calcium has two electrons in the shell closest to the nucleus. Explain why this is.

....

[1]
[Total 2 marks]

3 Electronic structures can be represented in different ways.

3.1 **Figure 1** shows the electronic structures of an atom of chlorine (Cl), and an atom of boron (B). Give the electronic structures of chlorine and boron in number form.

Chlorine: ....

Boron: ....

Figure 1

Chlorine   Boron

[2]

3.2 Sulfur has an atomic number of 16.
Complete the diagram to show the electronic structure of sulfur.

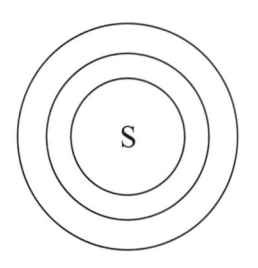

[2]
[Total 4 marks]

Exam Practice Tip

Electronic structures are a key idea in chemistry, so it's really important that you understand them. Definitely make sure you know, or can work out (by remembering how many electrons can fit into each electron shell), the electronic structures for the first 20 elements in the periodic table. Doing this will be really helpful for your exams.

Topic 1 — Atomic Structure and the Periodic Table

Development of The Periodic Table

1 In early periodic tables, scientists ordered elements by their atomic masses. The modern periodic table is ordered by atomic number.

1.1 Why were early periodic tables ordered by atomic mass and not atomic number?

....

....
[1]

1.2 State **two** problems with early periodic tables.

1. ....

2. ....
[2]
[Total 3 marks]

2 When Mendeleev arranged his periodic table, he left some gaps and also swapped the order of some elements. This meant the elements weren't ordered strictly by atomic mass.

2.1 Give **one** reason why Mendeleev arranged his table in this way.

....
[1]

2.2 How did the discovery of new elements help to show that the arrangement of Mendeleev's table was correct?

....

....
[1]

2.3 The discovery of which of the following things also helped to show that the arrangement of Mendeleev's table was correct?
Tick **one** box.

Neutrons ☐

Isotopes ☐

Atomic mass ☐

Molecules ☐
[1]
[Total 3 marks]

Exam Practice Tip

Mendeleev's table of the elements is a great example of Working Scientifically. Mendeleev came up with an idea, and later discoveries showed that he was right. Make sure you can explain what he did and why it was accepted by scientists.

Topic 1 — Atomic Structure and the Periodic Table

The Modern Periodic Table

1 Figure 1 shows the periodic table. *(Grade 3-4)*

Figure 1

1.1 How are the elements ordered in the periodic table?

....
[1]

1.2 What are the vertical columns in the periodic table called?

....
[1]

1.3 What type of elements are found in the shaded area labelled **A**?

....
[1]

[Total 3 marks]

2 Figure 2 shows the electronic configuration for atoms of three elements, **A**, **X** and **Z**. *(Grade 4-5)*

Figure 2

2.1 What group in the periodic table is element **X** in? Give a reason for your answer.

Group: ....

Reason: ....
[2]

2.2 Which period is element **X** in? Give a reason for your answer.

Period: ....

Reason: ....
[2]

2.3 Which **two** elements are in the same period?

....
[1]

2.4 Which element, **A** or **Z**, will react in a similar way to element **X**? Give a reason for your answer.

Element: ....

Reason: ....
[2]

[Total 7 marks]

Topic 1 — Atomic Structure and the Periodic Table

Metals and Non-Metals

1 About 80% of all the elements in the periodic table are metals. *Grade 3-4*

1.1 Describe where metals can be found in the periodic table.

....
[1]

1.2 Which **two** of the following properties are typical properties of metals?
Tick **two** boxes.

Conductors of electricity ☐

Liquids at room temperature ☐

Can be bent or hammered into different shapes ☐

Low density ☐

[1]
[Total 2 marks]

2 Some metals will react with particular non-metals to form compounds made of ions. *Grade 4-5*

2.1 Two elements, with the chemical symbols A and X, react together to form a compound made of A^{2+} ions and X^{2-} ions. One of the elements is a metal and one is a non-metal. State which element is the metal and which is the non-metal.

A^{2+} .... X^{2-} ....
[1]

2.2 Fill in the gaps to complete the passage about how metals react. Use the words in the box.

| gain | lose | share | half-full | full |

When metals react, they .... electrons.

When this happens they end up with a .... outer shell of electrons.
[2]

2.3 State **three** physical properties that non-metals are likely to have.

1. ....

2. ....

3. ....
[3]
[Total 6 marks]

Topic 1 — Atomic Structure and the Periodic Table

Group 1 Elements

1 The Group 1 elements show trends in their properties.

1.1 The density of the Group 1 elements **increases** down the group. Put the elements lithium (Li), sodium (Na) and potassium (K) in order from least dense to most dense.

.... Least dense

....

.... Most dense

[1]

1.2 Draw **one** line from each property to show how it changes as you go down Group 1.

Property   **Trend down Group 1**

Melting point   Increases

Boiling point   Decreases

                         Doesn't change

[2]

[Total 3 marks]

2 Lithium can react with chlorine.

2.1 What is the charge on the lithium ions that form in this reaction?

....

[1]

2.2 What type of compound is the product of this reaction?

....

[1]

[Total 2 marks]

3 This question is about the reactions of Group 1 elements with water.

3.1 Complete the word equation for the reaction of sodium with water:

sodium + water → .... + ...

[2]

3.2 Potassium reacts more strongly than sodium with water. Explain why.

....

....

....

....

[3]

[Total 5 marks]

Topic 1 — Atomic Structure and the Periodic Table

Transition Metals

1 Iron is a transition metal. It can react with chlorine, a non-metal, to form iron(III) chloride.

1.1 Potassium also reacts with chlorine. Which reaction is more vigorous? Tick **one** box.

   The reaction between iron and chlorine. ☐

   The reaction between potassium and chlorine. ☐

   Both reactions are equally vigorous. ☐

   There is not enough information given to be able to tell. ☐

   [1]

1.2 Many transition elements can form coloured compounds.
Which of the following statements are other properties of transition metals? Tick **two** boxes.

   They have low melting points compared to Group 1 metals. ☐

   They can form compounds which are good catalysts. ☐

   They are poor conductors of heat. ☐

   They can form more than one ion. ☐

   [2]

1.3 Which of the metals below are transition metals? Tick **two** boxes.

   ☐ nickel   ☐ magnesium   ☐ sodium   ☐ manganese

   [2]

   [Total 5 marks]

2 Copper and sodium are both metals.

2.1 Draw **one** line from each metal to the section of the periodic table it belongs with.

   Metal   **Section of the Periodic Table**

                            Group 1

   Sodium

                            Group 2

                            Transition Metals

   Copper

                            Group 7

   [2]

2.2 Using your knowledge of metals, describe **two** differences
in the physical properties of copper and sodium.

   ....

   ....

   ....

   [2]

   [Total 4 marks]

Topic 1 — Atomic Structure and the Periodic Table

Group 7 Elements

1 Complete the passage about the Group 7 elements. Use the words in the box.

| one | +1 | seven | −1 | eight |

The Group 7 elements all have .... electrons in their outer shell.

They can react to form ions with a .... charge.

[Total 2 marks]

2 The elements in Group 7 of the periodic table are known as the halogens.

2.1 Which of the following statements about the halogens is true? Tick **one** box.

They are non-metals that exist as single atoms. ☐

They are metals that exist as single atoms. ☐

They are non-metals that exist as molecules of two atoms. ☐

They are metals that exist as molecules of two atoms. ☐

[1]

2.2 Which halogen has the lowest boiling point?

....

[1]

[Total 2 marks]

3 This question is about the reactivity of the halogens.

3.1 Compare the chemical reactivity of chlorine and bromine. Explain your answer.

....

....

....

[3]

3.2 Halogens can react with other elements to form molecular compounds. Of the following elements, suggest which one might form a molecular compound with a halogen. Tick **one** box.

Na ☐   K ☐   H ☐   Cu ☐

[1]

Give a reason for your answer.

....

[1]

[Total 5 marks]

Topic 1 — Atomic Structure and the Periodic Table

Group 0 Elements

1 The Group 0 elements have similar properties. *Grade 3-4*

1.1 Describe the state of the Group 0 elements at room temperature.

....
[1]

1.2 Which of the following best describes the structure of the Group 0 elements?
Tick **one** box.

molecules containing two atoms ☐

single atoms ☐

ions ☐

metallic ☐

[1]

1.3 The Group 0 elements are unreactive. Explain why.

....
[1]

[Total 3 marks]

2 The noble gases can be found in Group 0 of the periodic table. *Grade 4-5*

2.1 Using the information in **Table 1**, complete the table by predicting the boiling point of radon (Rn).

Table 1

Element	Boiling Point / °C
Ar	−186
Kr	−152
Xe	−108
Rn	....

[1]

2.2 Explain the trend in boiling points as you go down Group 0.

....

....

....
[3]

[Total 4 marks]

Exam Practice Tip

You need to know why elements in Groups 1 and 7 are reactive and know what they react with. You also need to know why Group 0 elements don't react. Remember it's all about the number of electrons in the outer shell of the elements.

Topic 1 — Atomic Structure and the Periodic Table

Topic 2 — Bonding, Structure and Properties of Matter

Formation of Ions

1 This question is about ions. *(Grade 1-3)*

1.1 Complete the sentence below.
Use a word from the box.

atoms	electrons	charges

Ions are formed when .... gain or lose electrons.

[1]

1.2 An ion has a charge of +1.
How many electrons were lost in the formation of this ion?

....

[1]

[Total 2 marks]

---

2 This question is about ions and their formation. *(Grade 4-5)*

2.1 Which statement about the atoms of metallic elements is correct?
Tick **one** box.

Metal atoms usually lose electrons to become negative ions. ☐

Metal atoms usually gain electrons to become negative ions. ☐

Metal atoms usually gain electrons to become positive ions. ☐

Metal atoms usually lose electrons to become positive ions. ☐

[1]

2.2 There are four different ions shown below. Each one is of a different element.
Draw **one** line between each ion and its description.

Ion	Description
A$^+$	A non-metal from Group 6
D$^-$	A metal from Group 2
X^{2+}	A metal from Group 1
Z^{2-}	A non-metal from Group 7

[2]

[Total 3 marks]

Ionic Bonding

1 This question is about ionic bonding.

1.1 Ionic bonding involves metal and non-metal atoms bonding together.
Complete the sentences. Use words from the box.

| negatively | opposite | similar | neutrally | positively |

Metal atoms lose electrons to form .... charged ions.

The non-metal atoms gain electrons and form .... charged ions.

These ions have .... charges so they are attracted to each other.

[3]

1.2 Magnesium and oxygen bond together to form the ionic compound magnesium oxide (MgO).
To form MgO a magnesium atom **loses** two electrons and an oxygen atom **gains** two electrons.

State the formulas of the magnesium and oxygen ions in MgO.

Magnesium ion ....

Oxygen ion ....

[2]

[Total 5 marks]

2 The dot and cross diagram below shows the formation of lithium fluoride from its elements.

2.1 Complete the diagram by:
- adding an **arrow** to show the transfer of electron(s)
- adding the charges of the ions
- completing the outer shell electronic structure of the fluoride ion

[3]

2.2 Name the force that holds the ions together in an ionic bond.

....

[1]

2.3 State how you can tell from a dot and cross diagram that the particles in a compound are held together by ionic bonds.

....

[1]

[Total 5 marks]

Exam Practice Tip
Understanding how ionic compounds are formed can be a bit tricky. Just remember that no electrons disappear, they just move. Make sure you practise drawing some compounds with arrows to show how the electrons move and form the ions.

Ionic Compounds

Warm-Up

Circle the correct words or phrases in the passage below.

In an ionic compound, the particles are held together by weak/**strong** forces of attraction. These forces are called ionic bonds and act **in all directions**/in one direction.

1　Potassium bromide is an ionic compound made of potassium ions and bromide ions. *Grade 3-4*

　1.1　Complete the diagram below to show the position of the ions in potassium bromide. Write a symbol in each circle to show whether it is a potassium ion (K⁺) or a bromide ion (Br⁻).

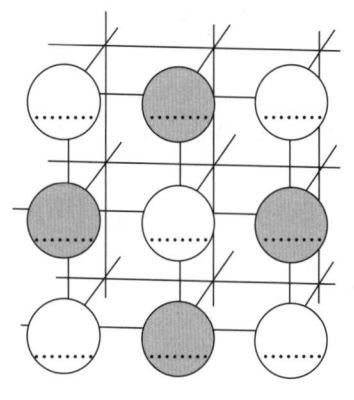

[1]

　1.2　Give **one** disadvantage of using the type of diagram above to show the structure of an ionic compound.

　　　..

　　　..
[1]
[Total 2 marks]

2　This question is about ionic compounds. *Grade 4-5*

　2.1　Which of the following properties is **not** typical for an ionic compound?
Tick **one** box.

　　　☐ high melting points　　　　☐ high boiling points

　　　☐ conduct electricity in the liquid state　　　☐ conduct electricity in the solid state
[1]

　2.2　Name the type of structure that ionic compounds have.

　　　..
[1]
[Total 2 marks]

Topic 2 — Bonding, Structure and Properties of Matter

Covalent Bonding

1 This question is about covalent bonding.

Complete the sentences. Use words from the box.

| metal | share | non-metal | covalent | electrons | swap |

Covalent bonds form between two .... atoms. These bonds form

because the atoms .... a pair of ....

[Total 3 marks]

2 The diagrams below show dot and cross diagrams of some covalent molecules.

2.1 Draw out the displayed formulas of these molecules using straight lines to represent covalent bonds. The displayed formula of molecule **A** has been done as an example.

Dot and cross diagram   **Displayed formula**

A   Cl — Cl

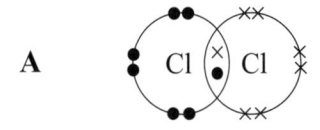

B

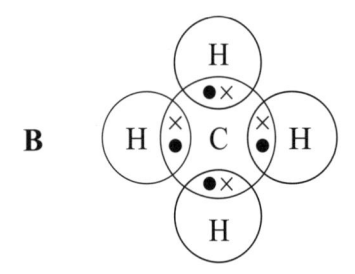

C

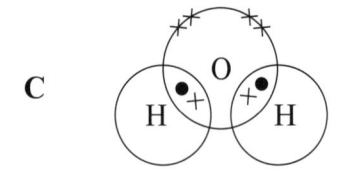

[2]

2.2 Write out the molecular formula for molecules **A**, **B** and **C**.

Molecule **A** ....

Molecule **B** ....

Molecule **C** ....

[3]

[Total 5 marks]

Topic 2 — Bonding, Structure and Properties of Matter

Simple Molecular Substances

1 **Figure 1** shows the electronic structures of hydrogen and oxygen atoms.

Figure 1

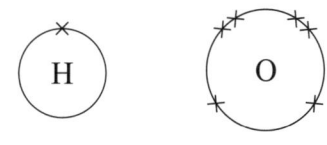

1.1 Complete the diagram below to show the shared electrons in a molecule of hydrogen (H₂).

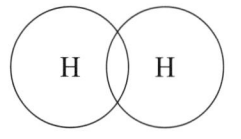

[1]

1.2 Complete the diagram below to show the shared electrons in a molecule of oxygen (O₂).

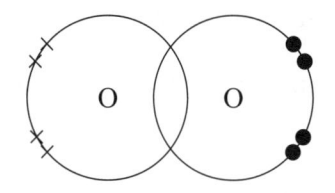

[1]
[Total 2 marks]

2 This question is about simple molecular substances.

2.1 Which of the molecules in **Table 1** is a simple molecular substance?

Table 1

Molecule	Molecular formula	Type of bonding
A	HCl	covalent
B	NaCl	ionic

Write your answer in the box.

[1]

2.2 Explain your answer to question 2.1.

....

....
[1]
[Total 2 marks]

Topic 2 — Bonding, Structure and Properties of Matter

3 Ammonia (NH₃) is a simple molecular compound.

3.1 Draw a dot and cross diagram to show a molecule of ammonia.
You should only show the outer shells of electrons.

[2]

3.2 Give **one** disadvantage of this type of diagram.

....
[1]
[Total 3 marks]

4 The bonds and forces in simple molecular substances have different strengths.

4.1 Compare the strength of the bonds that hold the atoms in a molecule
together with the forces that exist between different molecules.

....

....
[2]

4.2 When a simple molecular substance melts, is it the bonds between atoms
or the forces between molecules that are broken?

....
[1]

4.3 **Figure 2** shows two different simple molecular substances.

Figure 2

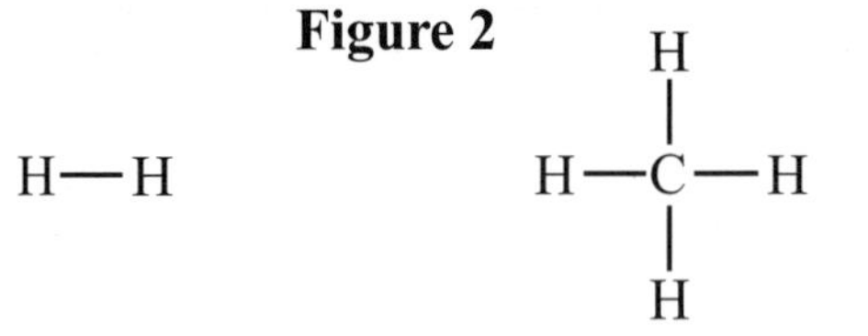

H—H

H—C—H with H above and H below

hydrogen   methane

Methane has a higher boiling point than hydrogen. Explain why.

....

....

....
[3]
[Total 6 marks]

Exam Practice Tip
It's a good idea to learn some examples of simple molecular substances — it'll help you remember what they are.
Keep in mind that they're small and have covalent bonds between atoms. Don't forget to learn their properties too.

Topic 2 — Bonding, Structure and Properties of Matter

Polymers and Giant Covalent Structures

Warm-Up

Complete the sentence below using words from the box.

| long | small | heavy | dense |

In a polymer lots of .... units are joined together to form a .... molecule.

1 Substances that contain covalent bonds can have very different structures. *Grade 1-3*

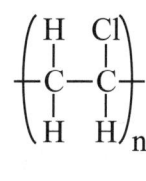

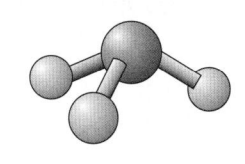

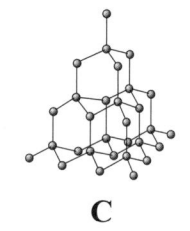

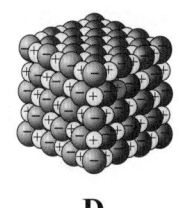

A B C D

Which diagram, **A**, **B**, **C** or **D**, represents a giant covalent structure? ....

[Total 1 mark]

2 This question is about giant covalent structures. *Grade 3-4*

2.1 Which of the following compounds is **not** an example of a giant covalent structure?
Tick **one** box.

☐ Ammonia   ☐ Diamond   ☐ Graphite   ☐ Silicon dioxide

[1]

2.2 Explain why most giant covalent compounds do not conduct electricity.

....
[1]
[Total 2 marks]

3 **Figure 1** represents a polymer. *Grade 4-5*

Figure 1

3.1 What is the molecular formula of this polymer?

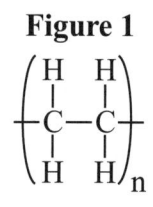

....
[1]

3.2 State what type of bonds hold the atoms in the polymer together.

....
[1]

3.3 Explain why most polymers are solid at room temperature.

....
[1]
[Total 3 marks]

Topic 2 — Bonding, Structure and Properties of Matter

Structures of Carbon

1 Several different carbon structures are shown in **Figure 1**.

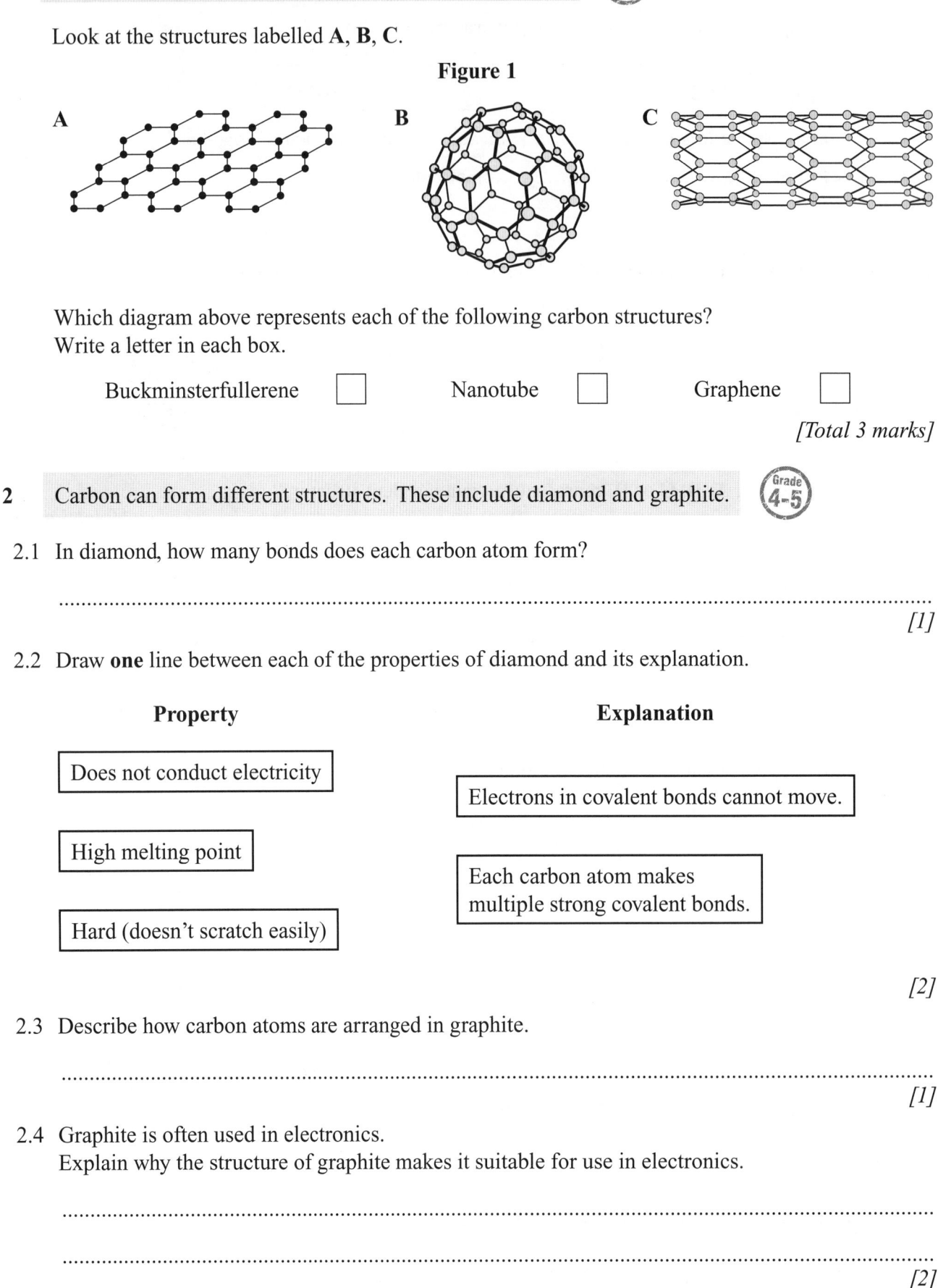

Look at the structures labelled **A**, **B**, **C**.

Figure 1

A B C

Which diagram above represents each of the following carbon structures?
Write a letter in each box.

Buckminsterfullerene ☐   Nanotube ☐   Graphene ☐

[Total 3 marks]

2 Carbon can form different structures. These include diamond and graphite.

2.1 In diamond, how many bonds does each carbon atom form?

....
[1]

2.2 Draw **one** line between each of the properties of diamond and its explanation.

Property	Explanation
Does not conduct electricity	Electrons in covalent bonds cannot move.
High melting point	Each carbon atom makes multiple strong covalent bonds.
Hard (doesn't scratch easily)	

[2]

2.3 Describe how carbon atoms are arranged in graphite.

....
[1]

2.4 Graphite is often used in electronics.
Explain why the structure of graphite makes it suitable for use in electronics.

....

....
[2]

[Total 6 marks]

Topic 2 — Bonding, Structure and Properties of Matter

Metallic Bonding

Warm-Up

Circle the elements shown below that are metals.

Copper   Nitrogen   Chlorine   Tin   Oxygen   Magnesium   Aluminium

1 Figure 1 shows two different metals. *(Grade 1-3)*

Which metal shown in **Figure 1** is an alloy?
Give a reason for your answer.

Metal ....

Reason ....

....

Figure 1 — Metal X, Metal Y

[Total 2 marks]

2 **Figure 2** shows the structure of a pure metal. *(Grade 4-5)*

2.1 In **Figure 2** some particles are labelled with an **X**.
Name these particles.

....
[1]

Figure 2 — X, metal ions

2.2 Metal atoms form ions that are positively charged.
Explain how they are held together in the structure seen in **Figure 2**.

....

....
[2]

2.3 Metals have high melting and boiling points. Explain why.

....

....
[2]

2.4 A scientist has samples of two different metals, **A** and **B**.
Metal A is pure iron. Metal B contains iron and other elements.
Which metal would you expect to be **easier** to bend? Explain your answer.

....

....

....
[3]

[Total 8 marks]

Topic 2 — Bonding, Structure and Properties of Matter

States of Matter

1 Look at the substances **A**, **B** and **C**, below.

A: NaCl₍s₎   **B**: O₂₍g₎   **C**: Hg₍l₎

1.1 Which substance is a solid? ☐

1.2 Which substance is a liquid? ☐

1.3 Which substance is a gas? ☐

[Total 3 marks]

2 Substances exist in one of the three states of matter. These are solids, liquids and gases. **Figure 1** shows how particles are arranged in each of the three states.

Figure 1

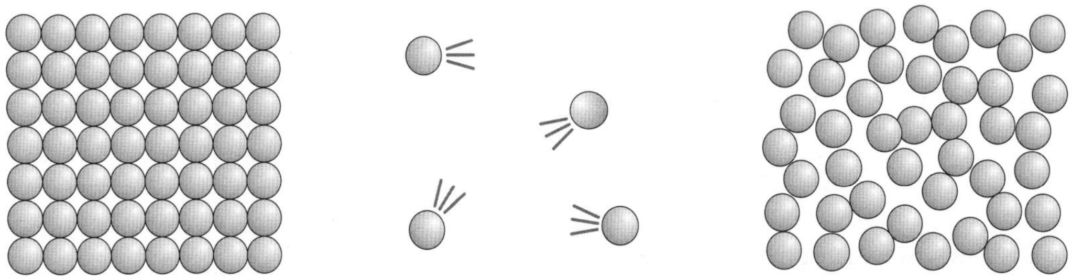

A   B   C

2.1 Which of the states shown in **Figure 1** represents a liquid? Give your answer as A, B or C.

....
[1]

2.2 In **Figure 1**, what does each ball represent?

....
[1]

[Total 2 marks]

3 The three states of matter are solids, liquids and gases.

3.1 Place solids, liquids and gases in order of the strength of attraction between their particles.

Strongest attraction   ....

                            ....

Weakest attraction   ....

[1]

3.2 When gases and liquids are placed inside a container they change shape. Why does this **not** happen when a solid is put inside a container?

....

....
[1]

[Total 2 marks]

Topic 2 — Bonding, Structure and Properties of Matter

Changing State

1 This question is about changing state.

In **Figure 1** the arrows represent processes that cause a change in state to happen.

Figure 1

Solid ←―A―― Liquid
      ――B―→

1.1 Process **A** causes a liquid to turn into a solid. Name this process.

....
[1]

1.2 Process **B** causes a solid to turn into a liquid. Name this process.

....
[1]

[Total 2 marks]

2 This question is about the processes by which a material changes state.

2.1 What is the name of the process when a liquid turns into a gas?

....
[1]

2.2 Liquid X turns into a gas at a very high temperature. What does this suggest about the strength of the forces of attraction between the particles in liquid X?

....
[1]

[Total 2 marks]

3 Use the data in **Table 1** to help you answer the questions that follow:

Table 1

Substance	Sodium Chloride	Water	Copper
Melting Point (°C)	801	0	1083
Boiling Point (°C)	1413	100	2567

3.1 Which substance in **Table 1** would be a liquid at 900 °C?

....
[1]

3.2 Which two substances in **Table 1** would be gases at 1500 °C?

....
[2]

[Total 3 marks]

Topic 2 — Bonding, Structure and Properties of Matter

Nanoparticles

Warm-Up

For each of the following statements, circle whether they are **true** or **false**.

1) Coarse particles have larger diameters than fine particles.   True or False

2) Nanoparticles have larger diameters than fine particles.   True or False

3) Atoms have smaller diameters than nanoparticles.   True or False

4) A particle with a diameter of 1000 nm would be classed as a fine particle.   True or False

5) Fine particles can also be called dust.   True or False

---

1 The surface area to volume ratio of an object can affect how it behaves. *Grade 4-5*

1.1 What is the volume of a cube with sides of 10 nm long? Tick **one** box.

☐ 1000 nm³   ☐ 600 nm³   ☐ 100 nm³   ☐ 10 nm³

[1]

1.2 What is the surface area of a cube with sides of 10 nm long? Tick **one** box.

☐ 1000 nm²   ☐ 600 nm²   ☐ 100 nm²   ☐ 10 nm²

[1]

1.3 How does the surface area to volume ratio of a cube change as its sides get longer?

....

....

[1]

[Total 3 marks]

---

2 Particles of matter can be sorted into categories based on how large they are. Draw lines to link each of the following statements on the left-hand side with the correct number on the right-hand side. *Grade 4-5*

| The maximum size, in nanometres (nm), of a nanoparticle. | 5000 |

| An approximate number of atoms present in one nanoparticle. | 500 |

| The possible size, in nanometres (nm), of a dust particle. | 100 |

[Total 2 marks]

Topic 2 — Bonding, Structure and Properties of Matter

Uses of Nanoparticles

1 The properties of some nanoparticles are listed in **Table 1**.

Table 1

Nanoparticle	Properties
Carbon nanotubes	Forms a cage-like structure that can be used to trap small molecules. Light and very strong.
Gold	Changes colour depending on the concentration of other compounds in solution.
Silver	Kills bacteria.

Suggest which material could be used for the following applications.
You can use each material more than once, and you do not need to use every material.

1.1 Delivering drugs to specific parts of the body.

....
[1]

1.2 Disinfecting water in a water filter.

....
[1]

1.3 Strengthening light-weight sports equipment, such as tennis racket strings.

....
[1]
[Total 3 marks]

2 Nanoparticles of zinc oxide are used in some sun creams to improve the protection of skin from exposure to sunlight.

2.1 State two possible advantages of using nanoparticles of zinc oxide in sun creams.

....
....
[2]

2.2 State two possible disadvantages to using nanoparticles of zinc oxide in sun creams.

....
....
[2]
[Total 4 marks]

Exam Practice Tip
You could be asked about nanoparticles that you haven't heard of — but don't panic. You'll be given any information you need for the question. You might need to use this information to say why a nanoparticle's good or bad for a job.

Topic 2 — Bonding, Structure and Properties of Matter

Topic 3 — Quantitative Chemistry

Relative Formula Mass

1 The relative atomic mass of chlorine is 35.5. The relative atomic mass of hydrogen is 1.

1.1 Calculate the relative formula mass of hydrochloric acid (HCl).

Relative formula mass = ...
[1]

1.2 Calculate the relative formula mass of chlorine gas (Cl_2).

Relative formula mass = ...
[1]
[Total 2 marks]

2 Match up the following formulas with the correct relative formula mass of the substance.

F_2	38
C_2H_6	40
CaO	30
NaOH	56

[Total 2 marks]

3 Magnesium oxide is a salt with the molecular formula MgO.
Relative atomic masses (A_r): O = 16, Mg = 24

3.1 Calculate the relative formula mass (M_r) of magnesium oxide.

Relative formula mass = ...
[1]

3.2 Calculate the percentage mass of magnesium in magnesium oxide.
Use the equation:

$$\text{Percentage mass of element in a compound} = \frac{A_r \text{ of element} \times \text{number of atoms of element}}{M_r \text{ of compound}} \times 100$$

Percentage mass of magnesium = ... %
[2]
[Total 3 marks]

Conservation of Mass

Warm-Up

The word equation for a reaction is shown below.

magnesium$_{(s)}$ + hydrochloric acid$_{(aq)}$ → magnesium chloride$_{(aq)}$ + hydrogen$_{(g)}$

1) Draw circles around the reactants in the equation above.
2) Draw boxes around the products in the equation above.
3) Which of the substances in the reaction is a gas? ....
4) Which of the substances is most likely to escape from the reaction container? ....

1 Iron and sulfur react together to produce iron sulfide. *(Grade 1-3)*

1.1 Which statement is correct? Tick **one** box.

Some mass will be lost in the reaction. ☐

The mass of the substances will increase during the reaction. ☐

The mass of the reactants will be the same as the mass of the products. ☐
[1]

1.2 28 g of iron reacts with 16 g of sulfur.
How much iron sulfide is made? Tick **one** box.

28 g of iron sulfide. ☐   16 g of iron sulfide. ☐   44 g of iron sulfide. ☐
[1]
[Total 2 marks]

2 Sodium hydroxide reacts with hydrochloric acid to produce sodium chloride and water. *(Grade 3-4)*
The equation is: sodium hydroxide + hydrochloric acid → sodium chloride + water

2.1 In an experiment, 80.0 g of sodium hydroxide reacted with 73.0 g of hydrochloric acid. 36.0 g of water was produced. Calculate the mass of sodium chloride produced.

Mass = ... g
[1]

2.2 The experiment was repeated using 109.5 g of hydrochloric acid. 175.5 g of sodium chloride and 54.0 g of water were produced. Calculate the mass of sodium hydroxide that reacted.

Mass = ... g
[1]
[Total 2 marks]

Topic 3 — Quantitative Chemistry

3 A student burned 12 g of magnesium in oxygen to produce magnesium oxide.

3.1 Which of the following is the correctly balanced equation for the reaction between magnesium and oxygen? Tick **one** box.

Mg + O → MgO ☐   2Mg + O$_2$ → 2MgO ☐

Mg + O$_2$ → 2MgO ☐   Mg + O$_2$ → MgO ☐

[1]

3.2 The student measured the mass of magnesium oxide produced. The mass was 20 g. Calculate the mass of oxygen that reacted with the magnesium.

Mass of oxygen = ... g
[1]
[Total 2 marks]

4 A student heated some sodium carbonate powder, as shown in **Figure 1**. When heated, sodium carbonate breaks down to produce sodium oxide and carbon dioxide.

The student measured the mass of the reaction container at the start and at the end of the reaction. The measurements the student took are shown in **Figure 2**.

Figure 1

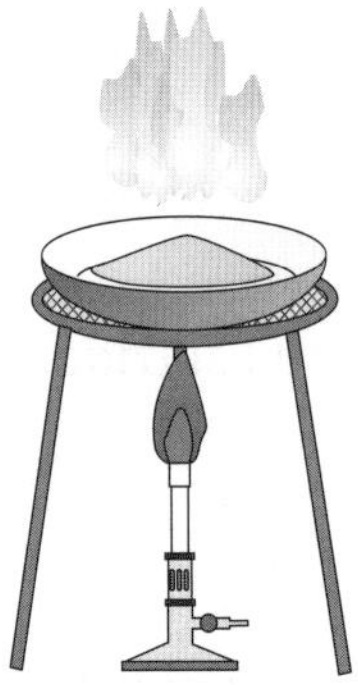

Figure 2

mass at the start of the reaction — 25.4

mass at the end of the reaction — 23.2

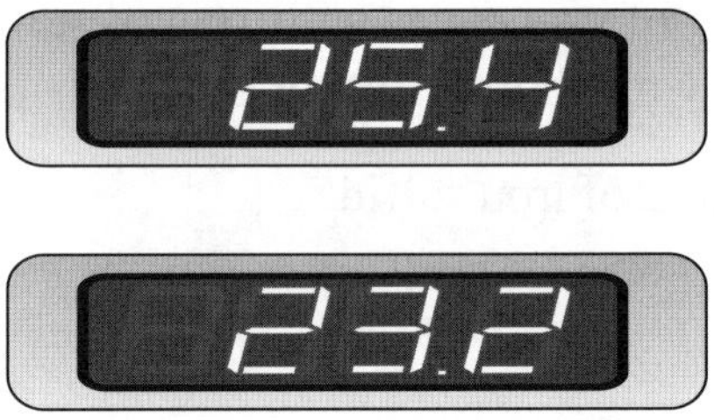

4.1 Calculate the change in mass of the reaction container during the reaction.

Change in mass = ... g
[1]

4.2 The student thinks that the measurements must be wrong, because no mass is lost or gained in a chemical reaction. Is the student correct? Explain your answer.

....
....
....
....
....

[4]
[Total 5 marks]

Topic 3 — Quantitative Chemistry

Concentrations of Solutions

Warm-Up

Some units are listed in the table on the right.

Put a tick in the correct column to show whether each unit is a unit of mass or a unit of volume.

Unit	Mass	Volume
g		
cm³		
dm³		
kg		

What is 0.5 dm³ in cm³? .... cm³

What is 750 cm³ in dm³? .... dm³

1 This question is about solutions.

Complete the sentences. Use words from the box.

| more | dissolved | less | crystallised | filtered |

When a solid is .... in a liquid, a solution is formed.

The greater the mass of the solid, the .... concentrated the solution.

The larger the volume of liquid, the .... concentrated the solution.

[Total 3 marks]

2 28 g of calcium chloride was dissolved in 0.4 dm³ of water.

2.1 Calculate the concentration of the solution and give the units.

Concentration = ... Units = ...
[2]

2.2 Explain the term 'concentration of a solution'.

....

....
[1]

2.3 A student needs another solution of calcium chloride, this time with a concentration of 50 g/dm³. What mass of calcium chloride do they need to add to 200 cm³ of water to make this solution?

Mass = ... g
[3]

[Total 6 marks]

Exam Practice Tip

For questions about concentrations, you'll probably need the formula that links concentration, mass and volume. It's a good idea to write down this formula triangle before you start. Then cover up the thing you want to find to work out how to calculate it from the values you do know.

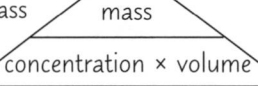

Formula triangle: mass / (concentration × volume)

Topic 3 — Quantitative Chemistry

Atom Economy

1 Ethene (C_2H_4) is often produced by heating ethanol (C_2H_5OH) with a catalyst. The equation for this reaction is: $C_2H_5OH \rightarrow C_2H_4 + H_2O$. Atomic masses ($A_r$): C = 12, H = 1, O = 16.

Grade 4-5

1.1 Calculate the relative formula mass of ethanol.

M_r of ethanol = ...
[1]

1.2 Calculate the relative formula mass of ethene.

M_r of ethene = ...
[1]

1.3 The percentage atom economy for a reaction is calculated using:

$$\frac{\text{Relative formula mass of desired product from equation}}{\text{Sum of relative formula masses of all reactants from equation}} \times 100\%$$

Calculate the atom economy of the reaction.

Atom economy = ... %
[2]

[Total 4 marks]

2 Atom economy measures the proportion of starting materials that form useful products.

Grade 4-5

2.1 State the atom economy for the following reaction: $CH_3OH + CO \rightarrow CH_3COOH$

....
[1]

2.2 How does the reaction equation suggest that this reaction has a high sustainability?

....
[1]

[Total 2 marks]

3 A student attempts to make sodium chloride (NaCl) using the following reaction: $CH_3ONa_{(aq)} + HCl_{(aq)} \rightarrow CH_3OH_{(l)} + NaCl_{(aq)}$

Grade 4-5

Calculate the atom economy of this reaction. Give your answer to 3 significant figures.
Relative formula masses (M_r): CH_3ONa = 54, HCl = 36.5, NaCl = 58.5

Atom economy = ... %
[3]

[Total 3 marks]

Topic 3 — Quantitative Chemistry

Percentage Yield

1 A student produced magnesium oxide by burning magnesium in air.
The student calculated the theoretical yield of magnesium oxide to be 2.4 g.
The actual yield of magnesium oxide was 1.8 g.

1.1 Calculate the percentage yield.

Percentage yield = ... %
[2]

1.2 The student's method involved heating a piece of magnesium of known mass in a crucible until the reaction appeared to have finished. The product was then tipped onto a balance and weighed. Suggest one way that this method may have decreased the percentage yield.

....

[1]
[Total 3 marks]

2 Ammonia is produced in the Haber process by reacting nitrogen gas with hydrogen gas.
The balanced symbol equation for this reaction is: $N_{2(g)} + 3H_{2(g)} \rightleftharpoons 2NH_{3(g)}$

2.1 A factory expected to produce 17 kg of ammonia. Only 4.5 kg were produced.
Calculate the percentage yield.

Percentage yield = ... %
[2]

2.2 Suggest two reasons why the actual yield of ammonia was lower than the maximum theoretical mass.

....

....

[2]
[Total 4 marks]

3 A student expected a reaction to produce 14.4 g of a product.

The percentage yield of the reaction was 30%. What mass of the product was produced?
Tick **one** box.

☐ 0.432 g   ☐ 4.32 g   ☐ 4.80 g   ☐ 0.48 g

[Total 1 mark]

Topic 3 — Quantitative Chemistry

Topic 4 — Chemical Changes

Acids and Bases

Warm-Up

Fill in the gaps in the following statements.

acids   bases   neutral

Substances with a pH of less than 7 are ....
Substances with a pH of more than 7 are ....
Substances with a pH of 7 are ....

1 This question is about acids and bases. **Table 1** shows some everyday substances. *Grade 3-4*

Table 1

Substance	Beer	Bicarbonate of Soda	Milk
pH	4	9	7

1.1 Write the name of the substance in **Table 1** that is an acid.

....
[1]

1.2 What colour would you expect universal indicator to turn in bicarbonate of soda solution?

....
[1]

[Total 2 marks]

2 The pH of a solution tells you how acidic or alkaline it is. *Grade 4-5*

2.1 Which ion is produced by an acid in aqueous solution? Tick **one** box.

Cl⁻ ☐   H⁺ ☐   OH⁻ ☐   OH⁺ ☐
[1]

2.2 State the range of the pH scale.

....
[2]

[Total 3 marks]

3 Acids and alkalis react together in neutralisation reactions. *Grade 4-5*

3.1 Write the word equation for a neutralisation reaction between an acid and an alkali.

.... + ... → .... + ...
[1]

3.2 Write an equation that shows how hydrogen (H⁺) and hydroxide (OH⁻) ions react together in a neutralisation reaction.

.... + ... → ....
[1]

3.3 State the pH of the products that form when an acid reacts with an alkali.

....
[1]

[Total 3 marks]

Topic 4 — Chemical Changes

Titrations

PRACTICAL

Warm-Up

Label the diagram using the labels below. The first one has been done for you.

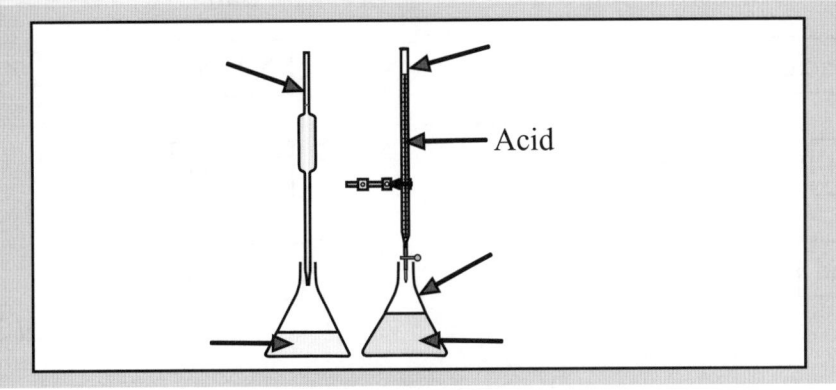

Solution containing alkali and an indicator
Alkali
~~Acid~~
Burette
Pipette
Conical flask

1   A student carries out a titration to measure the volume of alkali needed to neutralise a known volume of acid. *Grade 4-5*

1.1   Identify which of the following statements is false. Tick **one** box only.

Universal indicator is the most suitable indicator for use in titrations. ☐

Titrations can also be used to measure the volume of acid needed to neutralise a known volume of alkali. ☐

A pipette accurately measures a fixed volume of liquid. ☐

An indicator is usually used to identify the point of neutralisation in an acid-base titration. ☐

[1]

1.2   Explain why a burette is useful for identifying the end-point of a titration.

....
....
....
[2]

1.3   Here is the method the student uses for the titration:

1. Record the volume of alkali in the burette at the start. Slowly add the alkali to the acid from the burette. Swirl the flask regularly as you add the alkali.
2. Record the volume of alkali left in the burette at the end-point.
3. Calculate the volume of alkali added.

Explain how the method should be changed to increase the accuracy of the results.

....
....
[2]

[Total 5 marks]

Topic 4 — Chemical Changes

Reactions of Acids

1 Draw **one** line from each acid to the type of salt it forms when it reacts with a base.

Acid   **Salt**

Hydrochloric acid   Nitrate

Nitric acid   Sulfate

Sulfuric acid   Chloride

[Total 2 marks]

2 Acids react with metal carbonates.

2.1 Which of the following substances is **not** produced when a metal carbonate reacts with an acid?
Tick **one** box.

Salt ☐   Carbon dioxide ☐   Hydrogen ☐   Water ☐

[1]

2.2 A student adds 2 spatulas of zinc carbonate into a beaker of dilute hydrochloric acid. The student sees that the reaction fizzes. What product causes the reaction to fizz?

....

[1]

[Total 2 marks]

3 Sulfuric acid reacts with lithium hydroxide to produce lithium sulfate and one other product.

3.1 Name the product, other than lithium sulfate, that is produced in this reaction.

....

[1]

3.2 Which of the equations below is the balanced symbol equation for the reaction between lithium hydroxide and sulfuric acid?
Tick **one** box.

$2LiOH + H_2SO_4 \rightarrow Li_2SO_4 + 2H_2O$ ☐

$Li_2O + H_2SO_4 \rightarrow Li_2SO_4 + H_2O$ ☐

$Li_2O + H_2SO_4 \rightarrow Li_2SO_4 + H_2$ ☐

$2LiOH + H_2SO_4 \rightarrow Li_2SO_4 + H_2$ ☐

[1]

[Total 2 marks]

Topic 4 — Chemical Changes

4 The salt produced when an acid reacts with a metal hydroxide depends on the reactants.

4.1 Complete **Table 1** to show the salts that are formed when the acids and hydroxides react together.

Table 1

		Acid	
		Hydrochloric acid	Sulfuric acid
Metal hydroxide	Calcium hydroxide	Calcium chloride	....
	Copper hydroxide	....	....
	Magnesium hydroxide	....	....

[2]

4.2 Write a word equation for the reaction between hydrochloric acid and calcium hydroxide.

.... + ... → .... + ...

[1]

4.3 Complete and balance the symbol equation for the reaction between hydrochloric acid and calcium hydroxide.

Ca(OH)$_2$ + ... HCl → CaCl$_2$ + ... H$_2$O

[1]

[Total 4 marks]

5 Soluble metal salts can be made from the reactions of acids and metal oxides.

PRACTICAL

5.1 A student makes a soluble salt by reacting zinc oxide with hydrochloric acid. Name the salt that is produced.

....

[1]

5.2 Write a method that could be used to produce pure crystals of the salt using this reaction.

- Describe how you would make the salt from the reactants.
- Describe how you would purify the salt from the reaction mixture.

....
....
....
....
....
....
....

[4]

[Total 5 marks]

Topic 4 — Chemical Changes

The Reactivity Series and Extracting Metals

1   **Figure 1** shows part of the reactivity series of metals. Carbon has also been included in this reactivity series.

Figure 1

Potassium	K
Magnesium	Mg
Carbon	C
Copper	Cu

1.1 Name **one** metal from **Figure 1** that is more reactive than magnesium.

....
[1]

1.2 Name **one** metal from **Figure 1** which could be extracted from its ore by reduction with carbon.

....
[1]

1.3 Which metal in **Figure 1** forms positive ions most easily?

....
[1]

[Total 3 marks]

2   Iron can be extracted from its ore by reduction with carbon. The equation for this reaction is shown below.

$$2Fe_2O_3 + 3C \rightarrow 4Fe + 3CO_2$$

2.1 What is reduction?

....
[1]

2.2 Which element is oxidised in this reaction? Give a reason for your answer.

Element: ....

Reason: ....
[2]

2.3 Explain why magnesium **cannot** be extracted from its ore by reduction with carbon.

....

....
[1]

[Total 4 marks]

Exam Practice Tip

Learning the order of the reactivity series could be really useful when it comes to answering questions in the exams. Try learning this mnemonic to help you remember... Papa Smurf Likes Calling My Clarinet Zany — Isn't He Cute. (You don't have to use my Booker prize winning version, though. You could also make up your own.)

Reactions of Metals

1   What is the word equation for the reaction of a metal and an acid?
    Tick **one** box.

    metal + acid → salt + water ☐

    metal + acid → salt + hydrogen ☐

    metal + acid → metal hydroxide + hydrogen ☐

    metal + acid → salt + water + hydrogen ☐

    [Total 1 mark]

2   A student reacts different metals with water.
    The results of this experiment are shown in **Table 1**.

    Table 1

Reaction	Observation
Copper + water	No reaction
Calcium + water	Fizzing, calcium disappears
Lithium + water	Very vigorous reaction with fizzing, lithium disappears
Magnesium + water	No fizzing, a few bubbles on the magnesium

2.1 Write the word equation for the reaction of calcium and water.

    .... + ... → .... + ...
    [1]

2.2 Use **Table 1** to put the metals copper, calcium, lithium and magnesium in order of reactivity.

    Most reactive .... Least reactive
    [2]

2.3 State one thing the student should do to make sure the experiment is fair.

    ....
    [1]

2.4 The student then adds a piece of magnesium to a solution of copper chloride.
    A displacement reaction takes place. Predict the products of this reaction.

    ....
    [2]

2.5 State how you can predict whether a displacement reaction will take place between a metal and a metal compound.

    ....
    [1]

    [Total 7 marks]

Topic 4 — Chemical Changes

Electrolysis

Warm-Up

Place the labels on the correct label lines to identify the parts of an electrochemical cell.

Electrode   Electrolyte

D.C. power supply

1 Electrochemical cells contain electrodes in an electrolyte. The electrolyte can be a liquid or a solution.

Grade 3-4

1.1 Why does the electrolyte need to be a liquid or a solution? Tick **one** box.

So the ions can move to the electrodes ☐

So the electrons can be conducted through the substance ☐

So the electrodes don't corrode ☐

So there is enough heat for the reaction to occur ☐

[1]

1.2 Complete the passage below about electrodes. Use the words in the box. You can use words more than once.

positive   anode   cathode   gain   negative   lose   neutral

In electrolysis, the anode is the .... electrode. .... ions

move towards the anode and lose electrons. The cathode is the ....

electrode. .... ions move towards the cathode and gain electrons.

[4]

[Total 5 marks]

2 Lead bromide can be electrolysed. The electrolyte is molten lead bromide.

Grade 4-5

2.1 What is an electrolyte?

....

[1]

2.2 Write the word equation for the electrolysis of lead bromide.

.... → .... + ...

[1]

[Total 2 marks]

Topic 4 — Chemical Changes

3 Aqueous iron chloride solution can be electrolysed using inert electrodes. *Grade 4-5*

3.1 Which of the following ions are **not** present in iron chloride solution? Tick **one** box.

☐ Cl⁻   ☐ Fe²⁺   ☐ OH⁻   ☐ O²⁻

[1]

3.2 Explain why hydrogen, not iron, is formed at the cathode.

....

[1]

3.3 State what element is formed at the anode.

....

[1]

3.4 **Figure 1** shows the apparatus used to carry out the electrolysis of aqueous iron chloride solution.

Figure 1

PRACTICAL

Test tubes   Inert electrodes   Power supply   Beaker

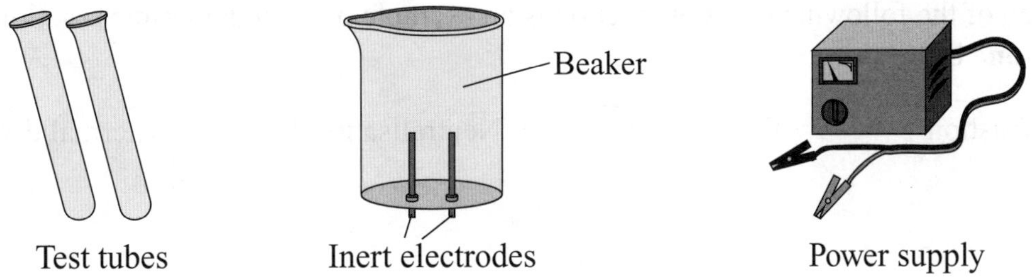

Outline how the apparatus in **Figure 1** could be used to collect any gases produced during electrolysis.

....
....
....
....
....
....
....

[4]
[Total 7 marks]

Exam Practice Tip

Remember, when you electrolyse a salt solution, different substances form at the electrodes depending on how reactive they are. If the metal's <u>more</u> reactive than hydrogen, hydrogen will form. If the metal's <u>less</u> reactive than hydrogen, the metal will form. At the anode, water and oxygen form unless there are halide ions (e.g. Cl⁻, Br⁻) in the solution.

Topic 4 — Chemical Changes

Topic 5 — Energy Changes

Exothermic and Endothermic Reactions

1 Complete the following definition of an exothermic reaction. Use the words in the box.

| takes in | gives out | rise | fall |

An exothermic reaction is one that .... energy.

This is shown by a .... in the temperature of the surroundings.

[Total 2 marks]

2 Chemical reactions result in a transfer of energy.

2.1 Compare the amount of energy stored in the products and reactants in an exothermic reaction.

....
[1]

2.2 Which of the following types of reaction is an example of an endothermic reaction?
Tick **one** box.

Combustion ☐   Oxidation ☐   Neutralisation ☐   Thermal decomposition ☐

[1]
[Total 2 marks]

3 During a reaction between solutions of citric acid and sodium hydrogen carbonate, the temperature of the surroundings went down.

3.1 How can you tell the reaction is endothermic?

....
[1]

3.2 Where is energy transferred from in an endothermic reaction?

....
[1]

3.3 What happens to the amount of energy in the universe after the reaction?

....
[1]

3.4 Give a practical use of this reaction.

....
[1]
[Total 4 marks]

Exam Practice Tip

The 'en' in 'endothermic' sounds like 'in', and the 'do' is the start of 'down'. So endothermic reactions take energy <u>in</u> from the surroundings, and make the temperature of the surroundings go <u>down</u>. Exothermic reactions do the opposite.

Topic 5 — Energy Changes

Measuring Energy Changes — PRACTICAL

1 A student investigated the temperature change of the reaction between sodium hydroxide and hydrochloric acid. The student set up the equipment as shown in **Figure 1**.

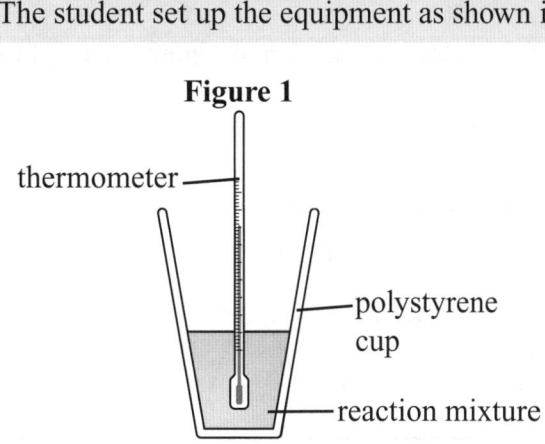

Figure 1

(diagram: thermometer in polystyrene cup containing reaction mixture)

1.1 Suggest **one** way the student should change the set-up shown in **Figure 1** in order to make the results more accurate. Give a reason for your answer.

Change: ....

Reason: ....
[2]

1.2 The student carried out the experiment using the method described in the steps below. Write a number 1, 2, 3 or 4 next to each step to put them in the correct order.

Step	Step number
Calculate the temperature change.	....
Mix the reactants together.	....
Measure the temperature of the reactants.	....
Measure the maximum temperature reached by the reaction mixture.	....

[2]

1.3 The results of the experiment are shown in **Table 1**.

Table 1

Initial Temperature (°C)	Final Temperature (°C)
18	31

Calculate the temperature change of the reaction.

Temperature change = ... °C
[1]

1.4 The student repeated the experiment a number of times using a different concentration of acid each time. State the independent and dependent variables in this experiment.

Independent: ....

Dependent: ....
[2]
[Total 7 marks]

Topic 5 — Energy Changes

Reaction Profiles

1 For a reaction to happen, particles need to collide with enough energy. *Grade 3-4*

1.1 What is the name given to the minimum amount of energy needed for a reaction to take place?

....
[1]

1.2 **Figure 1** shows the reaction profile of a reaction.

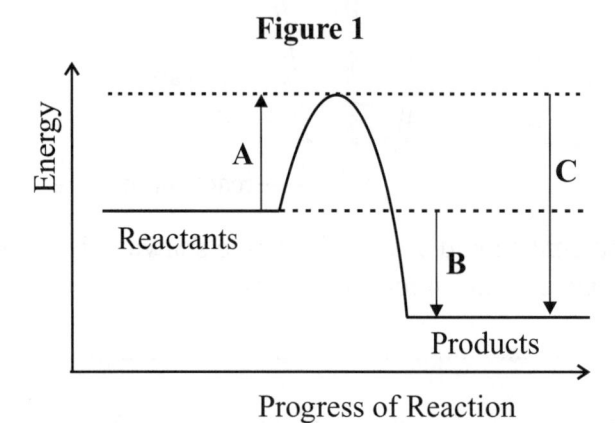

Figure 1

Which letter, **A**, **B**, or **C**, shows the amount of energy needed for the reaction to take place?

....
[1]

[Total 2 marks]

2 A reaction profile shows the overall energy change of a reaction. *Grade 4-5*

2.1 **Figure 2** shows the reaction profile for a reaction. Mark the overall energy change on **Figure 2**.

Figure 2

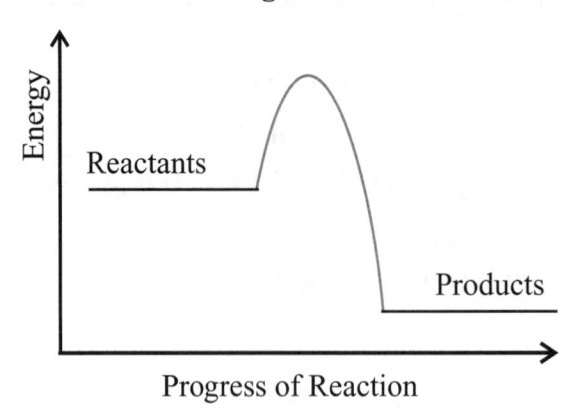

[1]

2.2 What type of reaction is represented by **Figure 2**? Give a reason for your answer.

Type of reaction: ....

Reason: ....
[2]

[Total 3 marks]

Topic 5 — Energy Changes

Cells, Batteries and Fuel Cells

Warm-Up

For each of the following statements, circle whether they are **true** or **false**.

1) A hydrogen fuel cell can be recharged. — True or False
2) The by-products from hydrogen fuel cells are water and carbon dioxide. — True or False
3) Alkaline batteries can't be recharged. — True or False

1 Draw lines from the chemicals below to the best description of the role they play in a hydrogen fuel cell. Draw **two** lines.

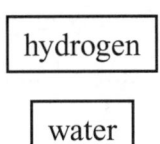

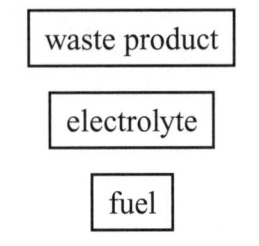

hydrogen   waste product
water   electrolyte
            fuel

[Total 2 marks]

2 A student was investigating chemical cells. They set up the following two cells shown in **Figure 1**.

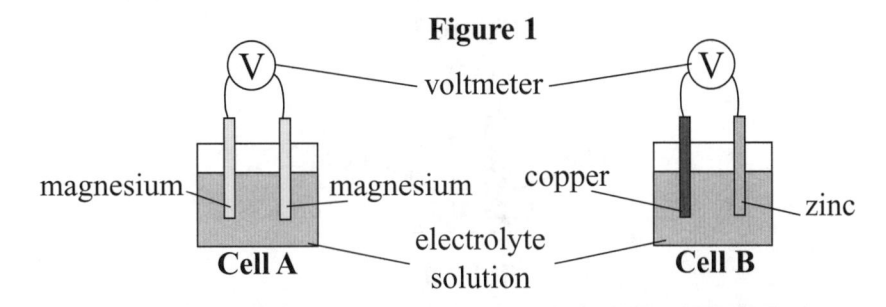

Figure 1

Cell A: magnesium — magnesium, electrolyte solution, voltmeter
Cell B: copper — zinc, electrolyte solution, voltmeter

2.1 The difference in reactivity between the electrodes determines the voltage of the cell. A larger difference in reactivity leads to a greater voltage. Which cell produces a greater voltage?

....
[1]

2.2 A student uses cell **B** to power a light bulb. Why does the light bulb eventually go out?
Tick **one** box.

☐ The electrons in the cell are used up so no voltage is produced.

☐ The reactants in the cell are used up so no voltage is produced.

☐ The products of the reaction in the cell are gases.

☐ The liquid in the cell evaporates so no voltage is produced.

[2]
[Total 3 marks]

Topic 5 — Energy Changes

3 Hydrogen is used in fuel cells, as shown in **Figure 2**.

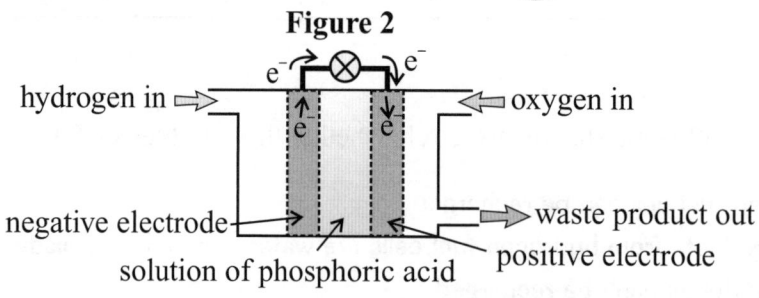

Figure 2

3.1 What happens to the hydrogen in a hydrogen fuel cell? Tick **one** box.

It is neutralised ☐   It is oxidised ☐   It is reduced ☐   It is decomposed ☐

[1]

3.2 Give **two** reasons why hydrogen fuel cells can be less polluting than rechargeable batteries.

....

....

....

[2]

[Total 3 marks]

4 A student investigated the reactivity of four unknown metals (labelled A to D) by using them as electrodes in simple cells as shown in **Figure 3**. The results are shown in **Table 1**.

Figure 3

Table 1

Metal 1	silver	silver	silver	silver
Metal 2	A	B	C	D
Voltage (V)	1.56	0.34	3.18	1.05

4.1 Which of the metals A-D is the most reactive? Tick **one** box.

A ☐   B ☐   C ☐   D ☐

[1]

4.2 The student builds a battery by connecting the cell which contains metal A to the cell which contains metal D. The cells are connected in series. Calculate the voltage of the battery.

Voltage = ... V

[1]

4.3 Which of the following does **not** affect the voltage of the cell? Tick **one** box.

electrolyte ☐   distance between electrodes ☐   type of electrode ☐

[1]

[Total 3 marks]

Topic 5 — Energy Changes

Topic 6 — The Rate and Extent of Chemical Change

Rates of Reaction

1 Collision theory can be used to explain the rate of a reaction.

1.1 According to collision theory, what **two** things will cause the rate of a reaction to increase? Tick **two** boxes.

The particles colliding more often. ☐

The particles colliding less often. ☐

The particles colliding with more energy. ☐

The particles colliding with less energy. ☐

[2]

1.2 At what point in a reaction is the rate fastest?

....

[1]

[Total 3 marks]

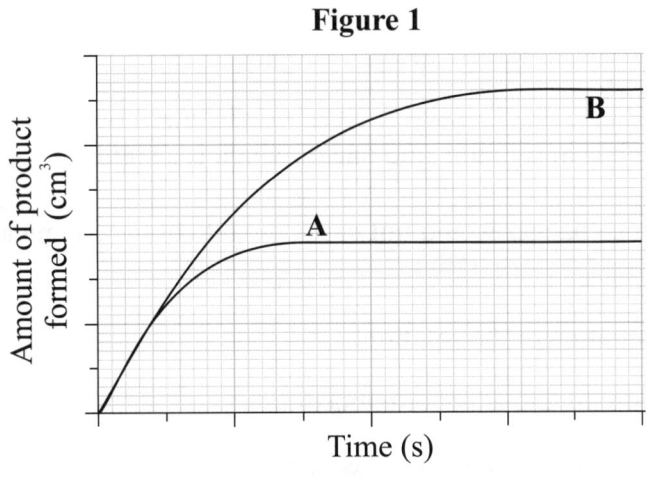

2 **Figure 1** shows how the volume of gas produced in a reaction changes over time, for the same reaction under different conditions, **A** and **B**.

Figure 1

[Graph: Amount of product formed (cm³) vs Time (s), showing two curves labelled A (lower plateau) and B (higher plateau)]

2.1 State whether reaction **A** or reaction **B** produced the most product.

....

[1]

2.2 What does it mean when the graph goes flat?

....

[1]

[Total 2 marks]

Factors Affecting Rates of Reaction

Warm-Up

A student reacts nitric acid with three different forms of calcium carbonate. All other variables are kept the same. Circle the condition that will result in the slowest rate of reaction.

lump of calcium carbonate   calcium carbonate chips   powdered calcium carbonate

---

1 A scientist carries out a reaction between two gases. *(Grade 3-4)*

The scientist repeats the experiment but decreases the pressure. All other reaction conditions are kept the same. Complete the paragraph by filling in the gaps. Use the words in the box below.

| decrease | more | increase | larger | less | smaller |

Increasing the pressure of the reaction will cause the rate of reaction to ....

This is because the same number of particles are in a .... space, so they will

collide .... frequently.

[Total 3 marks]

---

2 This question is about the rate of a chemical reaction between two reactants, one of which is in solution, and one of which is a solid. *(Grade 4-5)*

2.1 Which of the following changes would **not** cause the rate of the chemical reaction to increase? Tick **one** box.

Increasing the concentration of the solution. ☐

Heating the reaction mixture to a higher temperature. ☐

Using a larger volume of the solution, but keeping the concentration the same. ☐

Grinding the solid reactant so that it forms a fine powder. ☐

[1]

2.2 A catalyst is added to the reaction mixture and all other conditions are kept the same. The reaction rate increases. Explain why.

....

....

[1]

[Total 2 marks]

Topic 6 — The Rate and Extent of Chemical Change

Measuring Rates of Reaction — PRACTICAL

1 A certain reaction produces a gas product. Which **two** pieces of equipment below could be used to monitor the rate at which the gas is produced? Tick **two** boxes.

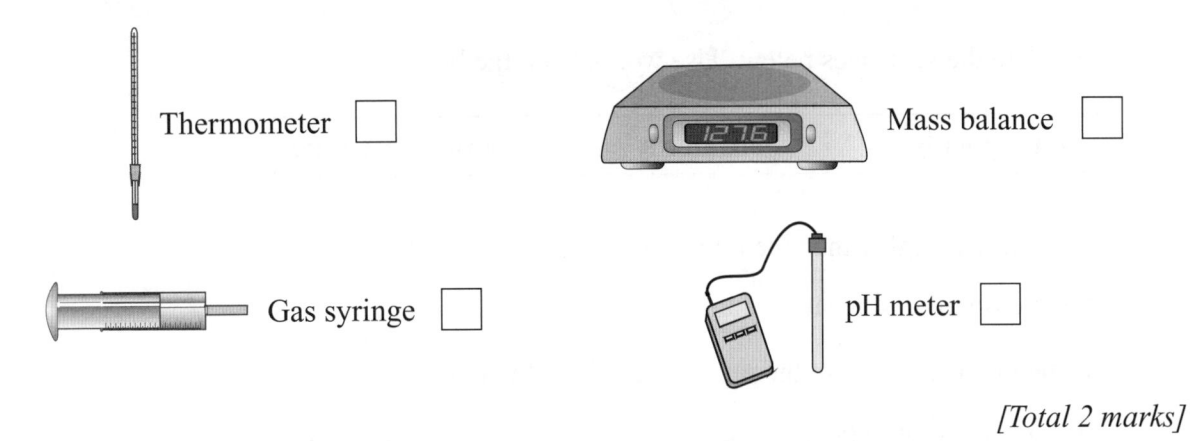

Thermometer ☐   Mass balance ☐

Gas syringe ☐   pH meter ☐

[Total 2 marks]

2 A student measures the volume of gas produced by the reaction between sulfuric acid and marble chips. He repeats the experiment with two different concentrations of acid, **A** and **B**. **Table 1** shows his results.

Table 1

		\multicolumn{6}{c}{Time (s)}
		0	10	20	30	40	50
Volume of gas produced (cm³)	Concentration A	3	8	10	12	16	19
	Concentration B	9	19	25	29	32	35

2.1 State the concentration, **A** or **B**, which resulted in the fastest reaction. Give a reason for your answer.

Concentration: ....

Reason: ....

....
[2]

2.2 What are the dependent and independent variables in this experiment?

Independent variable: ....

Dependent variable: ....
[2]

2.3 Suggest **one** variable that would have to be controlled in this experiment to make it a fair test.

....
[1]

[Total 5 marks]

PRACTICAL — More on Measuring Rates

1 A student carries out a reaction in a conical flask. She measures the time it takes for a black cross placed under the flask to disappear as a precipitate is formed. Under different conditions, the rate of the reaction changes.

Complete the sentences below. Use words from the box.

| more quickly | more slowly | in the same time |

If the rate is higher than the rate of the original reaction,

the cross will disappear ....

If the rate is lower than the rate of the original reaction,

the cross will disappear ....

[Total 2 marks]

2 A student investigates how the concentration of acid affects the rate of reaction between hydrochloric acid and sodium thiosulfate. The reaction forms a yellow precipitate. Her experimental set up is shown in **Figure 1**.

Figure 1

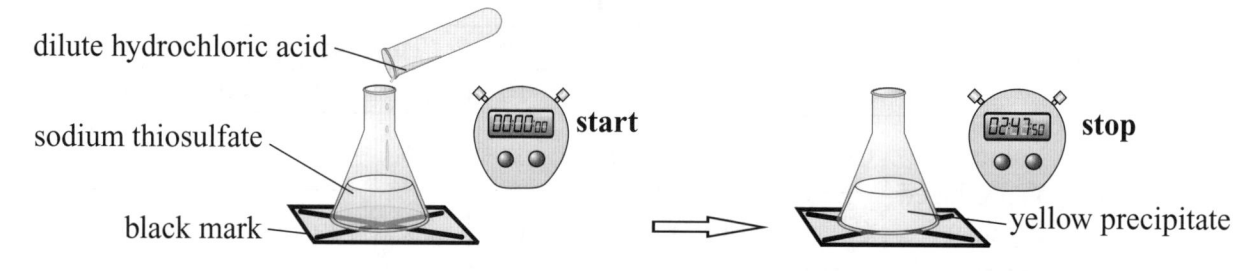

She uses five different acid concentrations and records how long it takes for the mark to disappear. All other variables are kept the same. Some of her results are shown in **Table 1**.

Table 1

Concentration of hydrochloric acid (g/dm³)	15	30	45	....	75
Time taken for mark to disappear (s)	....	187	....	174	168

2.1 Use the answers from the box below to complete **Table 1**.

| 90 | 181 | 165 | 60 | 194 |

[3]

2.2 Another student was observing these reactions but got different results to the first student. Suggest **one** reason why they may have different results.

....

[1]

[Total 4 marks]

Topic 6 — The Rate and Extent of Chemical Change

Graphs of Reaction Rate Experiments

1. The rate of a reaction was investigated by measuring the volume of gas produced at regular intervals. The results are shown in **Table 1**.

Table 1

Time (s)	0	50	100	150	200	250	300
Volume of gas (cm^3)	0.0	9.5	14.5	16.0	16.5	16.5	16.5

1.1 Plot the data in **Table 1** on the axes below. Draw a curved line of best fit onto the graph.

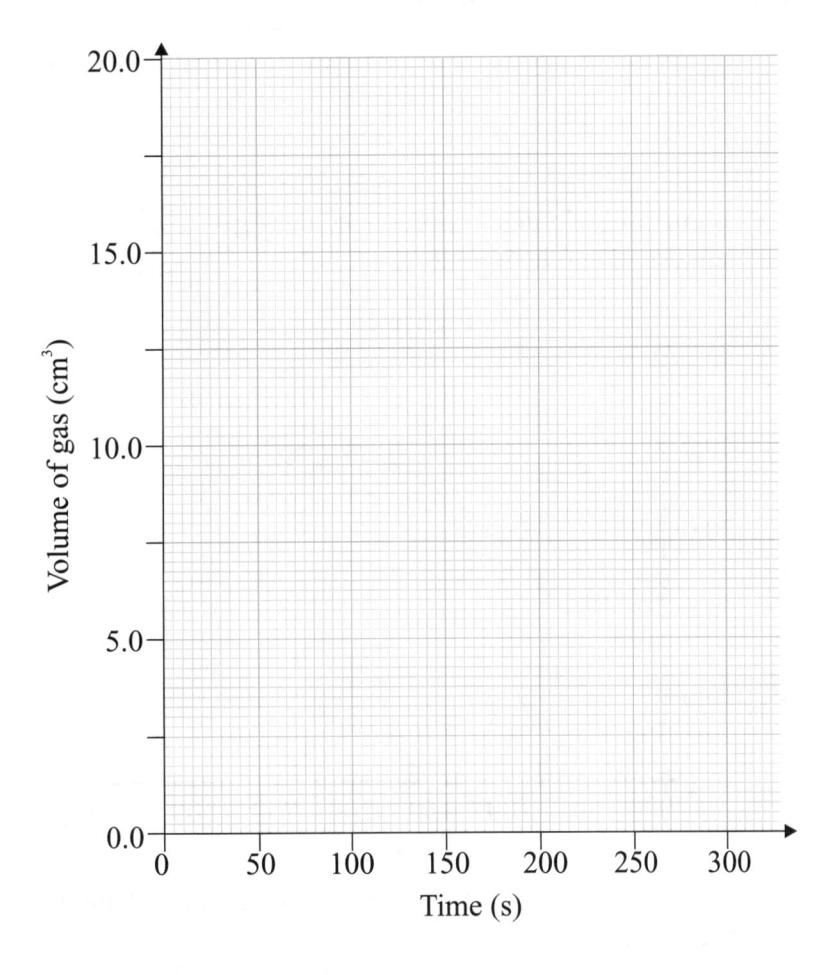

[3]

1.2 Draw tangents to the graph at 75 seconds and at 175 seconds.

[2]

1.3 Using the tangents drawn in part 1.2, state whether the reaction is fastest at 75 s or at 175 s. Give a reason for your answer.

Time: ....

Reason: ....

[2]

[Total 7 marks]

Exam Practice Tip
Plotting graphs can sometimes take a while, but make sure you take your time. It's easy to miss out a point or plot an x-value with the wrong y-value. You might be given a graph which doesn't have many values on the axis (like the graph's y-axis on this page). If so, feel free to add more values or markers to make it quicker and easier to plot your graph.

Topic 6 — The Rate and Extent of Chemical Change

Working Out Reaction Rates

1 In a reaction that lasted 125 seconds, 40 cm³ of gas was produced.

1.1 Calculate the mean rate of the reaction. Use the equation:

$$\text{mean rate of reaction} = \frac{\text{amount of product formed}}{\text{time}}$$

.... units
[2]

1.2 What will be the units of the rate? Tick **one** box.

s/cm³ ☐   cm³/s ☐   s³/cm ☐   cm/s³ ☐

[1]

[Total 3 marks]

2 **Figure 1** shows the volume of hydrogen gas produced during a reaction between magnesium and hydrochloric acid.

Figure 1

(Graph: Volume of H₂ produced (cm³) vs Time (s))

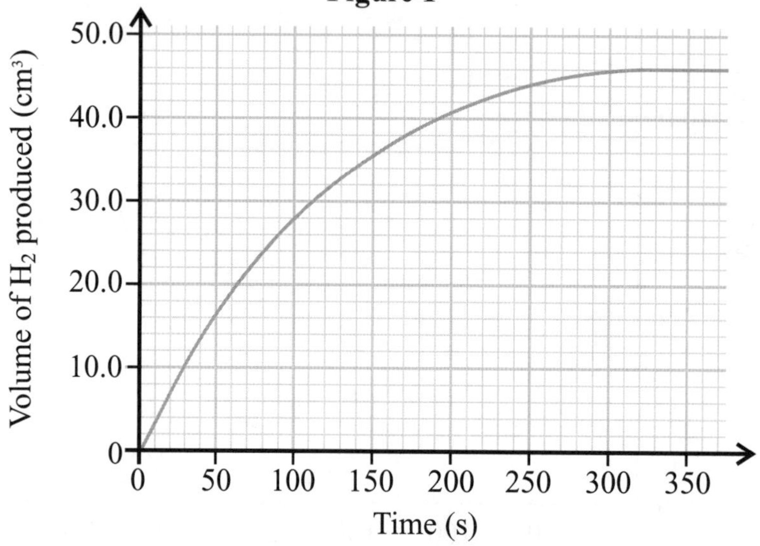

2.1 Calculate the mean rate for the whole reaction. Give your answer to 3 significant figures. Use **Figure 1** and the equation:

$$\text{mean rate of reaction} = \frac{\text{amount of product formed}}{\text{time}}$$

.... cm³/s
[2]

2.2 Calculate the mean rate of reaction between 100 seconds and 250 seconds. Give your answer to 3 significant figures.

.... cm³/s
[4]

[Total 6 marks]

Topic 6 — The Rate and Extent of Chemical Change

Reversible Reactions

1 Choose the symbol below that is used in a reaction equation to show that the reaction is reversible. Tick **one** box.

⇌ ☐   ⇄ ☐   ⇔ ☐   ↔ ☐

[Total 1 mark]

2 The two sentences below describe a reversible reaction. The forward reaction is endothermic and the backward reaction is exothermic. Complete the two sentences.

Use answers from the box.

| taken in | products | given out | the same as | reactants | different to |

1 When the reaction is cooled, it moves in the forward direction and

the amount of .... increases.

2 The energy .... by the endothermic reaction is ....

the amount .... during the exothermic reaction.

[Total 4 marks]

3 When a reversible reaction is carried out in a sealed container, it reaches equilibrium.

3.1 Which of the following statements about equilibrium is true? Tick **one** box.

At equilibrium, all the reactants have reacted to form products. ☐

At equilibrium, the amount of products equal the amount of reactants. ☐

At equilibrium, the rate of the forward reaction
is equal to the rate of the backwards reaction. ☐

At equilibrium, both the forwards and the backwards reactions stop. ☐

[1]

3.2 Suggest why carrying out this reaction in a sealed container means it can reach equilibrium.

....

....

[1]
[Total 2 marks]

Exam Practice Tip

When a reaction's at equilibrium, if there are more products than reactants, the reaction is going in the forwards direction. If there are more reactants than products at equilibrium, it's going in the backwards direction. But remember, the forward and backward reactions are going at the same rate and the amounts of products and reactants don't change.

Topic 6 — The Rate and Extent of Chemical Change

Topic 7 — Organic Chemistry

Hydrocarbons

1 The names of three alkanes (labelled **A**, **B** and **C**) are given below. **Figure 1** shows an alkane.

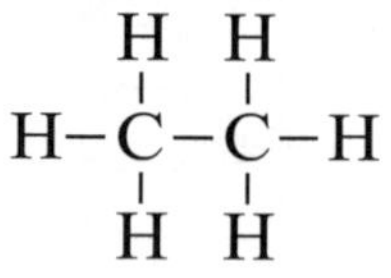

A ethane **B** propane **C** methane

Figure 1

H-C(-H)(-H)-C(-H)(-H)-H

1.1 What is the name of the alkane shown in **Figure 1**?
Write the letter **A**, **B** or **C** in the box.
[1]

1.2 Which alkane contains three carbon atoms?
Write the letter **A**, **B** or **C** in the box.
[1]
[Total 2 marks]

2 Alkanes are a family of hydrocarbons.

2.1 What is a hydrocarbon?
....
[2]

2.2 Complete the word equation for the complete combustion of an alkane.

alkane + oxygen → .... + ...
[1]

2.3 During a combustion reaction, the atoms in the alkane gain oxygen.
What is the name of this process?
....
[1]
[Total 4 marks]

3 The molecular formulas for five hydrocarbons, **A** to **E**, are shown below.

A C_4H_8 **B** C_4H_{10} **C** C_5H_{10} **D** C_5H_{12} **E** C_3H_8

3.1 Which of the hydrocarbons are alkanes? Explain your answer.
....
....
[2]

3.2 What is the name of hydrocarbon **B**?
....
[1]

3.3 Hydrocarbon **D** can be burned in air. Balance the equation for this reaction.

C_5H_{12} + ... O_2 → .... CO_2 + ... H_2O
[1]
[Total 4 marks]

Crude Oil

Warm-Up

Crude oil is used to make fuels for transport.
Circle the **four** substances below that are fuels made from crude oil.

diesel oil   petrol   kerosene   plastic   plankton   liquefied petroleum gas   oxygen   metal ores

1 This question is about crude oil. *(Grade 3-4)*

1.1 Complete the sentences below. Use words from the box.

| mud | finite | organic | renewable | plankton |

Crude oil is formed from .... and the remains of other plants and animals

that were buried in .... millions of years ago. Crude oil is being used up

much more quickly than it's being made, so it's a .... resource.

[3]

1.2 Substances made from crude oil are useful as fuels.
Give **two other** useful products that can be made from crude oil.

1 ....

2 ....

[2]

[Total 5 marks]

2 Crude oil is a resource that contains hydrocarbons. *(Grade 4-5)*

2.1 What property of hydrocarbons means that a large number of
different products can be made from crude oil? Tick **one** box.

Carbon can bond to all of the elements in the periodic table. ☐

Hydrogen atoms can bond with each other to form chains and rings. ☐

Carbon atoms bond together to form different groups of compounds. ☐

[1]

2.2 Different hydrocarbons have carbon chains of different lengths.
How does the boiling point of hydrocarbons change as the length of their carbon chains increases?

....

[1]

2.3 State **one** property of hydrocarbons, other than boiling point,
that changes as the length of the carbon chain increases.

....

[1]

[Total 3 marks]

Topic 7 — Organic Chemistry

Fractional Distillation

1   **Figure 1** shows a fractionating column.
They are used in the fractional distillation of crude oil. *(Grade 1-3)*

Figure 1

1.1   Where does crude oil enter the fractionating column?
Tick **one** box.

A ☐   B ☐   C ☐   D ☐   E ☐

[1]

1.2   Which is the hottest part of the fractionating column?
Tick **one** box.

A ☐   B ☐   C ☐   D ☐   E ☐

[1]

1.3   Where do the shortest hydrocarbons leave the fractionating column?
Tick **one** box.

A ☐   B ☐   C ☐   D ☐   E ☐

[1]

[Total 3 marks]

2   Before it enters the fractionating column, crude oil is heated until most of it evaporates. *(Grade 4-5)*

2.1   What change of state happens to the evaporated crude oil within the fractionating column?
Explain why this happens.

Change of state: ....

Explanation: ....

....

[2]

2.2*   In fractional distillation of crude oil, the hydrocarbons are separated out depending on the length of their carbon chains. Explain how this happens.

....

....

....

....

....

....

[6]

[Total 8 marks]

Exam Practice Tip

It's important to understand how a fractionating column works and why different substances drain out at different points.

Topic 7 — Organic Chemistry

Cracking

1 Crude oil is processed to make a variety of different products.

1.1 Long-chain hydrocarbons can be processed to produce short-chain hydrocarbons. What is the name of this process?

....
[1]

1.2 Name **two** types of hydrocarbons that are produced as a result of this process.

1 .... 2 ....
[2]

1.3 Why are long-chain hydrocarbons broken into shorter chain hydrocarbons?

....
[1]

[Total 4 marks]

2 Catalytic cracking and steam cracking can both be used to crack hydrocarbons.

2.1 Describe the method for steam cracking.

....

....
[2]

2.2 State one way in which the method for catalytic cracking is different to steam cracking.

....
[1]

2.3 Dodecane is an alkane with the formula $C_{12}H_{26}$. It can be cracked to produce heptane (C_7H_{16}) and one other hydrocarbon. Give the formula of this other hydrocarbon.

....
[1]

2.4 Dodecane can also be cracked to produce hexane (C_6H_{14}) and one other hydrocarbon. Balance the equation for cracking dodecane.

$$C_{12}H_{26} \rightarrow C_6H_{14} + 2C_{......}H_{......}$$
[1]

2.5 A scientist has a sample of hexane (an alkane) and a sample of pentene (an alkene). Describe a test that can be used to identify which sample is pentene. Include the test results that you would expect the scientist to see.

....

....

....

....
[3]

[Total 8 marks]

Topic 7 — Organic Chemistry

Alkenes

1 Alkenes form a homologous series of reactive organic compounds. *(Grade 3-4)*

1.1 Which of the following is the most accurate description of an alkene? Tick **one** box.

A hydrocarbon with a single carbon-carbon bond ☐

A hydrocarbon with a double carbon-carbon bond ☐

A hydrocarbon with a triple carbon-carbon bond ☐

A hydrocarbon with a double carbon-hydrogen bond ☐

[1]

1.2 What is the general formula for alkenes? Tick **one** box.

☐ C_nH_{n+2} ☐ C_nH_{2n+2} ☐ C_nH_{2n-2} ☐ C_nH_{2n}

[1]

1.3 Draw the displayed formula of propene, C_3H_6.

[1]

[Total 3 marks]

2 Five organic compounds, **A** to **E**, are shown in **Figure 1**. *(Grade 4-5)*

Figure 1

A: CH_4 (H-C-H with H above and below)
B: $CH_2=CH_2$
C: H-C-C-C-H (with H's, propane)
D: H-C-C-C-O-H (with H's, propanol)
E: $C=C$ with CH_3 and H groups

2.1 Which **two** of the molecules are unsaturated?

....
[1]

2.2 Give the molecular formula of **E**.

....
[1]

2.3 Alkenes burn in air with a smoky flame. State the type of combustion that occurs when alkenes burn in air. Complete the balanced equation for this reaction.

Type of combustion: ....

Balanced equation: .... C_2H_4 + ... O_2 → $2CO_2$ + ... $CO + 4H_2O$

[2]

[Total 4 marks]

Topic 7 — Organic Chemistry

Reactions of Alkenes

Warm-Up

Fill in the gaps for the following paragraph using the words below on the left.

alcohols   addition   unsaturated   bromine water   oxidation   ethene

Alkenes often react by the .... of atoms onto the carbons in the carbon-carbon double bond. Alkenes can react with steam to form .... For example, ... can be mixed with steam and passed over a catalyst to form ethanol.

1 Ethene is a hydrocarbon that takes part in addition reactions.

1.1 Circle the functional group of ethene in **Figure 1**.

Figure 1

[1]

1.2 Why does propene react in a similar way to ethene?

....
[1]

1.3 Complete the sentences below to describe what happens to the functional group in ethene during an addition reaction. Use words from the box.

| double | atom | single | hydrogens | carbons | bonds |

The double bond opens up to leave a .... bond.

A new .... is added to each of the ....

[3]
[Total 5 marks]

2 Alkenes can react with hydrogen gas to form alkanes. The reaction between propene and hydrogen is shown in **Figure 2**.

Figure 2

2.1 What is the molecular formula of propene?

....
[1]

2.2 What metal catalyst is added to speed up the reaction?

....
[1]

2.3 Bromine water is added to the organic reactant. Describe what observation would be seen.

....
[1]
[Total 3 marks]

Topic 7 — Organic Chemistry

3 Alkenes can react in an addition reaction with halogens. An example of the reactants that can take part in this type of reaction is shown in **Figure 3**.

Figure 3

3.1 Complete the displayed formula of X in **Figure 4** by adding any atoms that are needed.

Figure 4

H H H H
| | | |
H–C–C–C–C–H
| | | |

[1]

3.2 The product of this reaction is saturated. What does this mean?

....

....

[1]

[Total 2 marks]

4 Propene is a feedstock for the production of many useful organic compounds.

4.1 Propene reacts with iodine, I_2. Complete **Figure 5** by drawing the displayed formula of the product of the reaction between iodine and propene.

Figure 5

[1]

4.2 Propene also reacts with steam in the presence of a catalyst. There are two possible products of this reaction. The displayed formula of one of the possible products is shown in **Figure 6**. Draw the displayed formula of the other product.

Figure 6

H H H
| | |
H–C–C–C–H
| | |
H O H
 |
 H

[1]

[Total 2 marks]

Exam Practice Tip
Don't get in a tizz if you're asked about the reaction of an alkene with a reactant that you're unsure about. All you need to remember is that the double bond in the alkene is likely to react in the same way as it does in all the other reactions you've met. So keep a cool head, think about the general rules of alkene addition reactions and you'll be sorted.

Topic 7 — Organic Chemistry

Addition Polymers

Warm-Up

The sentences below are about addition polymers.
Circle **one** underlined word or phrase in each sentence, so that the sentence is correct.

> Polymers are large molecules which are made by joining together smaller molecules called <u>catalysts</u> / <u>monomers</u> / <u>repeating units</u>.
> Addition polymers can be formed from hydrocarbons called <u>alkanes</u> / <u>alkenes</u> / <u>halogens</u>.

1 Poly(ethene) is a polymer used in packaging applications.

1.1 What is the monomer used to form poly(ethene)? Tick **one** box.

☐ ethane ☐ ethene ☐ ethanol ☐ ethanoic acid

[1]

1.2 Give all the products formed in the polymerisation reaction that produces poly(ethene).

....
[1]

1.3 What functional group in the monomer reacts when poly(ethene) is made?

....
[1]

[Total 3 marks]

2 The displayed formula of the polymer poly(chloroethene) is shown in **Figure 1**.

Figure 1

$$\left(\begin{array}{cc} H & Cl \\ | & | \\ -C-C- \\ | & | \\ H & H \end{array} \right)_n$$

2.1 Draw the displayed formula of the monomer.

[1]

2.2 Name the monomer used to form poly(chloroethene).

....
[1]

[Total 2 marks]

Exam Practice Tip

Don't panic if you're asked to find the monomer from a repeating unit. The monomer of an addition polymer will always have a C=C double bond, so start by drawing that. Then look at the repeating unit for what groups surround it.

Topic 7 — Organic Chemistry

Naturally Occurring Polymers

1 There are several polymers that are important for life. *Grade 1-3*

1.1 What type of polymer is made up of amino acid monomers? Tick **one** box.

- [ ] polyester
- [ ] protein
- [ ] DNA
- [ ] RNA

[1]

1.2 What type of molecule are the monomers in starch? Tick **one** box.

- [ ] sugars
- [ ] amino acids
- [ ] alkenes
- [ ] nucleotides

[1]

1.3 Name **one** other naturally occurring polymer that is made up of the same type of monomers as starch.

....

[1]

[Total 3 marks]

2 DNA is a polymer found in every living thing. *Grade 4-5*

2.1 What is the main role of DNA? Tick **one** box.

- [ ] make enzymes
- [ ] store energy
- [ ] encode genetic instructions

[1]

2.2 Complete the sentences below to describe the general structure of DNA. Use words from the box.

| bonded | two | helix | four | monomers | atoms |

DNA contains .... polymer chains, which

are made from four different nucleotide ....

The polymer chains form a double .... structure.

[3]

[Total 5 marks]

Topic 7 — Organic Chemistry

Alcohols

1 This question is about alcohols.

1.1 Circle the functional group of butanol in **Figure 1**.

Figure 1

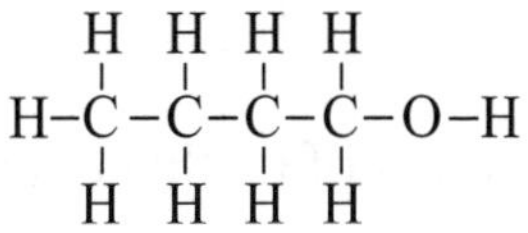

$$H-\underset{\underset{H}{|}}{\overset{\overset{H}{|}}{C}}-\underset{\underset{H}{|}}{\overset{\overset{H}{|}}{C}}-\underset{\underset{H}{|}}{\overset{\overset{H}{|}}{C}}-\underset{\underset{H}{|}}{\overset{\overset{H}{|}}{C}}-O-H$$

[1]

1.2 State **two** uses of alcohols.

....
[2]

1.3 A few drops of methanol are added to a test tube containing water and a few drops of universal indicator. What would you observe? Tick **one** box.

Two layers since methanol does not dissolve in water. The indicator remains green. ☐

Methanol dissolves. The indicator remains green. ☐

Methanol dissolves. The indicator turns orange. ☐

Methanol dissolves. The indicator turns blue. ☐

[1]

[Total 4 marks]

2 Ethanol is used as a starting material for other organic products. It can be made by fermenting sugar.

2.1 Ethanol can be oxidised to a carboxylic acid. Give the name of this carboxylic acid.

....
[1]

2.2 Complete the word equation for the fermentation of sugar.

sugar $\xrightarrow{\text{yeast}}$ ethanol + ...

[1]

2.3 What conditions are needed for the fermentation of sugar? Tick **one** box.

A temperature of 15 °C, high pressure and an acidic pH. ☐

A temperature of 37 °C, anaerobic conditions and a slightly acidic pH. ☐

A temperature of 100 °C and high pressure. ☐

A temperature of 450 °C and a pressure of 200 atmospheres. ☐

[1]

[Total 3 marks]

3 Methanol and butanol are both alcohols.

3.1 Complete the displayed formula of methanol in **Figure 2**.

Figure 2

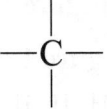

—C—

[1]

3.2 Give one difference between the structures of methanol and butanol.

....
[1]

3.3 What feature of methanol and butanol makes them both react in a similar way?

....
[1]

3.4 Both methanol and butanol can react with sodium. One of the products of the reaction is gaseous. What gas is produced in the reaction of methanol and butanol with sodium? Tick **one** box.

☐ carbon dioxide ☐ hydrogen ☐ oxygen ☐ carbon monoxide

[1]

3.5 Predict the pH of an aqueous solution of butanol.

....
[1]

[Total 5 marks]

4 Octanol is shown in **Figure 3**.

Figure 3

H H H H H H H H
| | | | | | | |
H–C–C–C–C–C–C–C–C–O–H
| | | | | | | |
H H H H H H H H

4.1 How could you produce hydrogen from octanol?

....
[1]

4.2 Balance the equation below which shows the complete combustion of octanol.

C$_8$H$_{17}$OH + ... O$_2$ → .... CO$_2$ + ... H$_2$O

[1]

[Total 2 marks]

Topic 7 — Organic Chemistry

Carboxylic Acids

1 Methanoic acid is the simplest carboxylic acid possible.

1.1 What is the functional group in methanoic acid?
Tick **one** box.

☐ –CH$_3$ ☐ C=C   ☐ –OH   ☐ –COOH

[1]

1.2 A few drops of methanoic acid are added to Universal indicator solution in a test tube. What colour will the Universal indicator turn? Tick **one** box.

☐ orange   ☐ green   ☐ blue   ☐ purple

[1]

1.3 Methanoic acid reacts with calcium carbonate. What gas is produced?

....
[1]
[Total 3 marks]

2 Carboxylic acid **A** is shown in **Figure 1**. It reacts with ethanol to form another organic compound.

Figure 1

H H H   O
| | | //
H–C–C–C–C
| | | \
H H H   O–H

2.1 Name carboxylic acid **A**.

....
[1]

2.2 Give the formula for carboxylic acid **A**.

....
[1]

2.3 What type of catalyst is used to increase the reaction rate in the reaction between carboxylic acid **A** and ethanol?

....
[1]

2.4 What type of compound is made by the reaction between the compound in **Figure 1** and ethanol?

☐ an alcohol   ☐ an alkene   ☐ a hydrocarbon   ☐ an ester

[1]
[Total 4 marks]

Topic 7 — Organic Chemistry

Topic 8 — Chemical Analysis
Purity and Formulations

1 A paint was made up of 20% pigment, 35% binder, 25% solvent, and 20% additives. *Grade 3-4*

1.1 Which of the statements below does **not** explain why the paint is a formulation? Tick **one** box.

It is a mixture that has been designed for a certain use. ☐

Each part contributes to the properties of the formulation. ☐

The mixture is made up of less than five parts. ☐

Each part of the mixture is present in a measured amount. ☐

[1]

1.2 Other than paint, name **one** example of a formulation.

....

[1]

[Total 2 marks]

2 This question is about purity. *Grade 4-5*

2.1 How is a pure substance defined in chemistry? Tick **one** box.

A single element not mixed with any other substance. ☐

A single compound not mixed with any other substance. ☐

A single element or compound not mixed with any other substance. ☐

An element that has not been reacted with anything. ☐

[1]

2.2 The melting point of two samples of copper were measured. Sample **A** had a melting point of 1085 °C and sample **B** melted over the range 900 – 940 °C. Suggest which of the two samples was pure. Explain your answer.

....

....

[2]

2.3 The boiling point of water is 100 °C.
A scientist adds some salt to a sample of water and measures the boiling point of the solution. How will the addition of salt affect the boiling point of the water?

....

[1]

[Total 4 marks]

Exam Practice Tip

A formulation is a mixture but a mixture isn't always a formulation. For the exam make sure you know what the difference is. Formulations are designed for a particular use and contain ingredients in specific amounts.

Topic 8 — Chemical Analysis

Paper Chromatography

Warm-Up

Use the words to label the different parts of the chromatography experiment shown on the right.

baseline   filter paper   spots of chemicals   solvent front

....

1   Paper chromatograms were produced for three dyes, **D**, **E** and **F**, using different solvents. **Figure 1** shows a chromatogram produced using ethanol as the solvent.

Figure 1

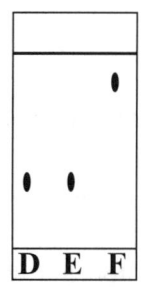

|D E F|

1.1   The chromatography experiment that produced the chromatogram in **Figure 1** had two phases. Which of the following statements describing the mobile phase is **true**? Tick **one** box.

The dyes moved in the mobile phase. ☐

The mobile phase was the filter paper. ☐

The stationary phase moved up the mobile phase. ☐

The least soluble dye spent a longer time in the mobile phase. ☐

[1]

1.2   Why do different substances travel different distances along the paper?

....

....
[1]

1.3   In all solvents, each dye only has one spot. What does this suggest about the dyes?

....
[1]

[Total 3 marks]

Topic 8 — Chemical Analysis

Using Chromatograms

PRACTICAL

1. A scientist used chromatography to analyse the composition of five food colourings. Four of the colourings were unknown (**A – D**). The other was sunrise yellow. The results are shown in **Figure 1**.

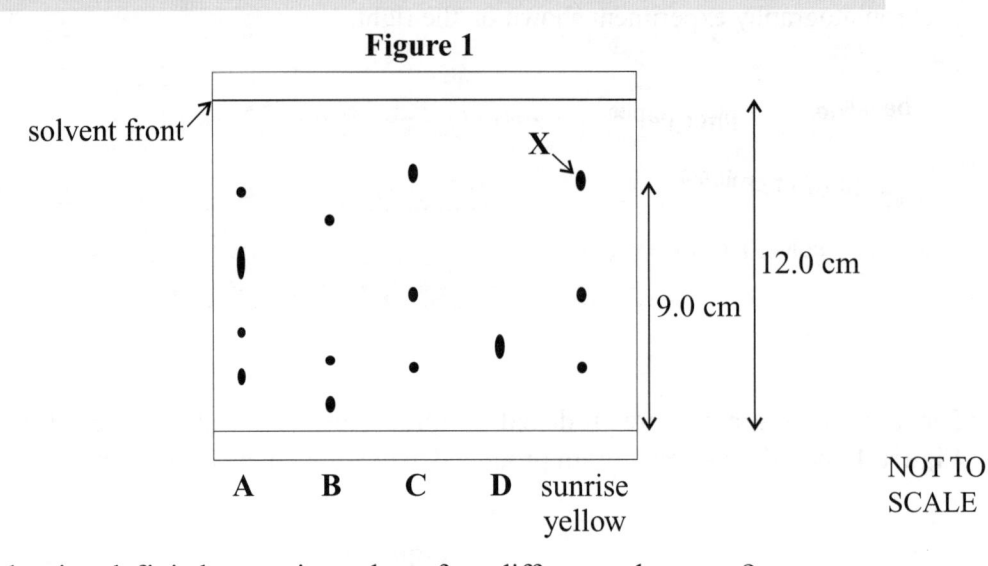

Figure 1

NOT TO SCALE

1.1 Which food colouring definitely contains at least four different substances?

....
[1]

1.2 Which of the food colourings, **A-D**, could be made of the same substances as sunrise yellow?

....
[1]

1.3 How could you check whether the food colouring you identified in question 1.2 is made of the same substances as sunrise yellow?

....

....

....
[2]

1.4 Calculate the R_f value for the spot of chemical labelled **X** in **Figure 1**.

Use the equation: $R_f = \dfrac{\text{distance moved by substance}}{\text{distance moved by solvent}}$

R_f = ...
[2]

1.5 Describe how the scientist could use chromatography to find out whether food colouring **A** contained a particular substance.

....

....

....
[2]

[Total 8 marks]

Topic 8 — Chemical Analysis

Tests for Gases

1 A student wants to identify a gaseous product.

Figure 1 shows the gas being tested.

Figure 1

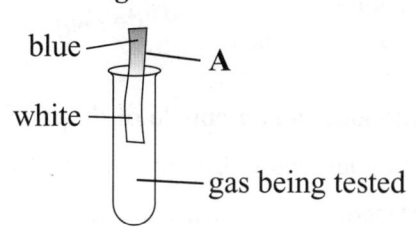

- blue — A
- white
- gas being tested

1.1 Name the item labelled **A** in **Figure 1**.

....
[1]

1.2 Suggest which gas was present in the test tube.

....
[1]
[Total 2 marks]

2 A student performs an experiment that produces a colourless gas. To identify the gas, she collects it and carries out tests.

2.1 Suggest why the student should perform the experiment in a fume cupboard.

....
[1]

2.2 The student bubbles some of the gas through limewater. What gas is this test used to identify?

....
[1]

2.3 When a lighted splint was placed into a sample of the gas, it was **not** accompanied by a popping sound. What does this tell you about the gas?

....
[1]

2.4 When the student placed a glowing splint into a sample of the gas, the splint relighted. Name the gas that was produced by her experiment.

....
[1]
[Total 4 marks]

Exam Practice Tip

There are only four tests for gases you need to know. But, you'll also need to know any precautions that need to be taken to carry out the tests safely. The test for carbon dioxide is also important for testing for carbonate ions.

Topic 8 — Chemical Analysis

Tests for Ions

PRACTICAL

Warm-Up

Fill in the gaps for the following paragraph using the words below.

cloudy   barium chloride   dilute acid   carbon dioxide   oxygen
lilac

To test for carbonate ions, add a couple of drops of ....
to a test tube of the substance. Connect the test tube to a test tube of limewater.
If a carbonate is present, ... will be given off and will
turn the limewater ....

1 Certain positive ions can be identified using flame tests. *Grade 3-4*

1.1 A flame test was conducted on a sample containing an unknown cation.
The sample burned with a green flame. Identify the unknown cation. Tick **one** box.

☐ Lithium, Li^+ ☐ Potassium, K^+ ☐ Copper, Cu^{2+} ☐ Calcium, Ca^{2+}

[1]

1.2 The method for conducting a flame test is shown below.
Complete the missing step in the method.

1) Clean a platinum wire loop by dipping it in some dilute HCl and then placing it in a blue flame from a Bunsen burner until it burns without colour.

2) ....
....

3) Record the colour of the flame.

[1]

1.3 A solution containing sodium ions was tested using a flame test.
What colour flame would you expect to see?

....

[1]

[Total 3 marks]

2 A student carried out tests to identify the compound present in a solution. *Grade 4-5*

2.1 The student added a couple of drops of hydrochloric acid
followed by a couple of drops of barium chloride to the solution.
A white precipitate was formed. What anion was present in the solution? Tick **one** box.

☐ Sulfate, SO_4^{2-} ☐ Carbonate, CO_3^{2-} ☐ Chloride, Cl^- ☐ Hydroxide, OH^-

[1]

Topic 8 — Chemical Analysis

2.2 The student added a few drops of aqueous sodium hydroxide to the solution. A green precipitate was formed. What cation was present in the solution? Tick **one** box.

☐ Sodium, Na⁺ ☐ Iron(II), Fe²⁺ ☐ Copper, Cu²⁺ ☐ Iron(III), Fe³⁺

[1]

2.3 Use your answer to 2.1 and 2.2 to identify the compound in solution.

....

[1]

[Total 3 marks]

3 Some simple chemical tests were carried out on two unknown substances in solution, **P** and **Q**. The results are shown in the **Table 1**.

Grade 4-5

Table 1

Substance	Flame test colour	Addition of sodium hydroxide, NaOH$_{(aq)}$	Addition of silver nitrate (AgNO$_3$)$_{(aq)}$ in the presence of nitric acid
P	orange-red	D	yellow precipitate
Q	E	blue precipitate	no reaction

3.1 What metal ion is present in substance **P**? Tick **one** box.

☐ Sodium, Na⁺ ☐ Potassium, K⁺ ☐ Copper, Cu²⁺ ☐ Calcium, Ca²⁺

[1]

3.2 State the observation for **D**.

....

[1]

3.3 What anion is present in substance **P**? Tick **one** box.

☐ Chloride, Cl⁻ ☐ Bromide, Br⁻ ☐ Iodide, I⁻

[1]

3.4 Identify substance **P**.

....

[1]

3.5 What metal ion is present in substance **Q**?

....

[1]

3.6 State the observation for **E**.

....

[1]

3.7 There is no reaction when silver nitrate is mixed with substance **Q**. What does this suggest about substance **Q**? Tick **one** box.

Substance **Q** contains a halide ion. ☐

Substance **Q** does not contain a halide ion. ☐

Substance **Q** is not a salt. ☐

Substance **Q** is not reactive. ☐

[2]

[Total 8 marks]

Topic 8 — Chemical Analysis

Flame Emission Spectroscopy

1 Flame emission spectroscopy is an example of an instrumental method that can be used to analyse elements and compounds. *Grade 3-4*

1.1 What are some advantages of using instrumental methods compared to chemical tests? Tick **two** boxes that are correct.

☐ more accurate   ☐ cheaper   ☐ simpler   ☐ faster

[2]

1.2 Flame emission spectroscopy can be used to identify the metal ions in a solution. What other information can flame emission spectroscopy tell you?

....
[1]

1.3 What type of spectra does flame emission spectroscopy produce?

....
[1]

[Total 4 marks]

2 Flame emission spectroscopy can be used to detect various positive ions within a mixture. **Figure 1** shows the spectra for Metal **A**, Metal **B**, Metal **C** and a mixture, **M**. *Grade 4-5*

Figure 1

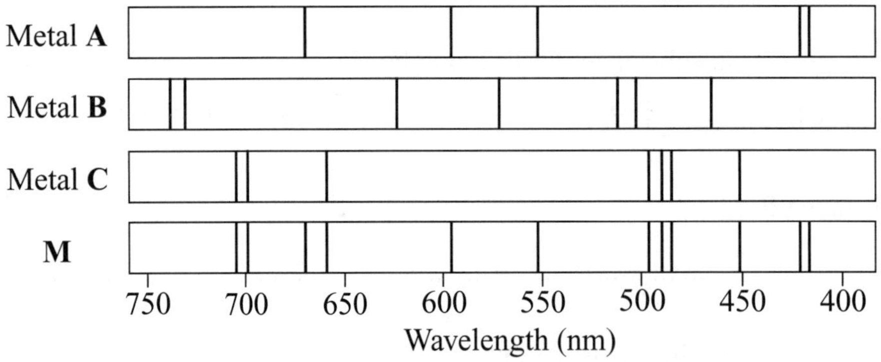

[Spectra diagram showing Metal A, Metal B, Metal C, and M against Wavelength (nm) from 750 to 400]

2.1 Complete the sentences below to describe how flame emission spectroscopy works. Use words from the box.

| ion | light | atom | energy | molecules | heat |

A sample is placed in a flame and as the ions in the sample heat up they

transfer .... as .... , which then passes through a

spectroscope and produces a line spectrum specific to that ....

[3]

2.2 Mixture **M** does not contain any ions from metal **B**. How can you tell?

....

....
[1]

[Total 4 marks]

Topic 8 — Chemical Analysis

Topic 9 — Chemistry of the Atmosphere

The Evolution of the Atmosphere

Warm-Up

Write the numbers 1-4 in the boxes below to put the events in the order in which they happened.

Animals evolved. ☐   The oceans formed. ☐

The early atmosphere formed. ☐   Plants evolved. ☐

---

1 The composition of gases in the atmosphere has varied during Earth's history. *(Grade 3-4)*

1.1 What are the approximate proportions of oxygen and nitrogen in the atmosphere today?
Tick **one** box.

Four-fifths oxygen and one-fifth nitrogen. ☐   Three-fifths oxygen and two-fifths nitrogen. ☐

One-fifth oxygen and four-fifths nitrogen. ☐   Two-fifths oxygen and three-fifths nitrogen. ☐

[1]

1.2 Other than oxygen and nitrogen, name **two** gases in the atmosphere today.

....

[2]

1.3 How was the oxygen in the atmosphere produced?

....

[1]

1.4 How was the nitrogen in the atmosphere produced?

....

[1]

[Total 5 marks]

2* Describe how the amount of carbon dioxide in the atmosphere got to the level that it is at today. *(Grade 4-5)*

Include ideas about:
- How carbon dioxide originally became part of the atmosphere.
- How the amount of carbon dioxide in the early atmosphere was different to how it is today.
- Reasons why the amount of atmospheric carbon dioxide has changed.

....

....

....

....

....

....

[Total 6 marks]

Greenhouse Gases and Climate Change

1 Greenhouse gases in the atmosphere help maintain life on Earth.

1.1 Which of the following is **not** a greenhouse gas? Tick **one** box.

Nitrogen ☐   Carbon dioxide ☐   Water vapour ☐   Methane ☐
[1]

1.2 Use the words in the box below to complete the paragraph describing the greenhouse effect.

| long | absorbed | cools | short | reflected | warms |

The sun gives out .... wavelength radiation.

The Earth reflects this as .... wavelength radiation.

This radiation is .... by greenhouse gases and then given out in all directions.

Some heads back to Earth and .... the Earth's surface.

[4]

[Total 5 marks]

2 **Figure 1** shows how the concentration of CO_2 in the atmosphere has changed over time.

Figure 1

2.1 Outline what **Figure 1** tells you about the concentration of atmospheric carbon dioxide.

....

....
[1]

2.2 Give **one** example of a type of human activity which has contributed to the change in atmospheric carbon dioxide concentration, shown in **Figure 1**.

....
[1]

2.3 Over the same time period, the global temperature has increased. Suggest **one** reason why it's hard to prove that the change in carbon dioxide is causing the increase in temperature.

....
[1]

2.4 Increased global temperature could cause climate change. Give **one** possible effect of climate change.

....
[1]

[Total 4 marks]

Topic 9 — Chemistry of the Atmosphere

Carbon Footprints

1 In recent years, governments and businesses have tried to reduce their carbon footprints.

1.1 The following statements describe some of the difficulties in reducing carbon footprints. Which of the statements is **false**? Tick **one** box.

Governments are worried that their economies will be affected if they try to reduce carbon footprints. ☐

Countries cannot always make agreements about reducing emissions. ☐

Governments are worried that reducing carbon footprints could lead to sea levels rising. ☐

Technologies with lower carbon footprints need more development. ☐

[1]

1.2 Complete **Table 1** to show whether each action would increase or decrease a carbon footprint. Tick **one** box in each row.

Table 1

Action	Increase	Decrease
Producing more waste		
Using more renewable energy resources		
Using more fossil fuels		
Using processes that require more energy		
Capturing carbon dioxide and storing it underground		

[3]

[Total 4 marks]

2 Individuals have an annual carbon footprint.

2.1 What is meant by the term 'carbon footprint'?

....

....

[2]

2.2 Suggest **two** reasons why an individual may not try to reduce their carbon footprint.

....

....

[2]

[Total 4 marks]

Exam Practice Tip
Learning the definitions for all the different terms that crop up in GCSE Science may be a bit of a bore, but it might be really useful in the exams. Learning all the itty bitty details is worth it if it means you get all the marks available.

Topic 9 — Chemistry of the Atmosphere

Air Pollution

1 Draw **one** line from each pollutant to show how it's formed.

Pollutant	How Pollutant is Formed
sulfur dioxide	Incomplete combustion of hydrocarbons.
nitrogen oxides	Reaction of gases in the air caused by the heat of burning fossil fuels.
particulates	Combustion of fossil fuels that contain sulfur impurities.

[Total 2 marks]

2 Some of the pollutants that are released when fuels burn can cause acid rain.

2.1 Name **one** pollutant that can lead to acid rain.

....
[1]

2.2 State **two** ways in which acid rain can be damaging.

1. ....

2. ....
[2]

[Total 3 marks]

3 Combustion of fuel in cars is a major contributor to air pollution.

3.1 Nitrogen oxides can be formed from the combustion of fuels in cars.
Give **two** problems caused by nitrogen oxides in the environment.

....

....
[2]

3.2 Fuel combustion can produce particulates. What impact do particulates have on human health?

....
[1]

3.3 Combustion of fuels can also produce a gas that prevents blood from carrying oxygen around the body. Inhaling it can cause health problems, and sometimes death.

Name the gas and give the reason why it is difficult to detect it.

Name: ....

Reason: ....
[2]

[Total 5 marks]

Topic 9 — Chemistry of the Atmosphere

Topic 10 — Using Resources

Ceramics, Polymers and Composites

1 This question is about the structures of polymers and composites. *Grade 3-4*

1.1 Low density poly(ethene) and high density poly(ethene) are both made from ethene. Which statement below explains why they have different properties? Tick **one** box.

☐ They are made at the same temperature and pressure with a different catalyst.

☐ They are made at different temperatures and pressures with the same catalyst.

☐ They are made at different temperatures and pressures with a different catalyst.

[1]

1.2 Poly(ethene) melts when it is heated. Is it a thermosetting or thermosoftening polymer?

....
[1]

1.3 What is meant by the term 'composite material'?

....

....
[2]

1.4 Name **one** example of a composite material.

....
[1]

[Total 5 marks]

2 There are many different types of ceramic with very different properties. For example, brick and glass are both ceramic materials. *Grade 4-5*

2.1 What three ingredients are used to make soda-lime glass?
Tick **three** boxes.

☐ Limestone ☐ Sand ☐ Salt ☐ Sodium hydroxide ☐ Sodium carbonate

[3]

2.2 Boiling tubes are used to heat liquids. Suggest why boiling tubes are made from borosilicate glass rather than soda-lime glass.

....
[1]

2.3 Briefly describe how bricks are made from clay.

....

....
[2]

[Total 6 marks]

Topic 10 — Using Resources

Properties of Materials

1 This question is about mixtures of different metals known as alloys.

Draw **one** line between each alloy and the mixture of elements that it contains.

Bronze		Copper and zinc
Steel		Copper and tin
Brass		Iron and carbon

[3]

[Total 3 marks]

2 This question is about gold and its alloys.

2.1 Complete the following passage using words from the box below.

| chromium | 24 | zinc | softer | 18 | harder |

Metals such as silver, ... and copper are added to gold to make it

.... Pure gold is described as .... carat gold.

[3]

2.2 What name is given to a gold alloy which contains 50% gold? Tick **one** box.

☐ 6 carat ☐ 12 carat ☐ 18 carat ☐ 24 carat

[1]

[Total 4 marks]

3 Table 1 shows some data about the properties of various steels.

Table 1

Alloy	Carbon Content (%)	Strength (MPa)
Stainless steel	0.08	205
Low carbon steel	0.1	245
High carbon steel	1.5	355

3.1 Use the data in **Table 1** to state the effect on strength of increasing the carbon content of steel.

....

[1]

3.2 Use the data in **Table 1** to suggest which alloy would be most suitable for building a bridge. Give your reasoning.

Alloy: ....

Reason: ....

[2]

[Total 3 marks]

Topic 10 — Using Resources

Corrosion

1 Iron reacts with water and oxygen to form hydrated iron(III) oxide, known as rust. *Grade 3-4*

1.1 Write the word equation for the formation of rust.

....

[1]

1.2 An electrochemical cell can be used to coat iron with a protective layer of metal that doesn't corrode. What is this process called? Tick **one** box.

☐ galvanisation ☐ electroplating ☐ sacrificial protection

[1]

1.3 Explain how this process prevents iron from rusting.

....

....

[1]

[Total 3 marks]

2 This question is about corrosion in metals and how to prevent it. *Grade 4-5*

2.1 What does the term 'corrosion' mean?

....

....

[1]

2.2 Corrosion is not a problem for objects made from aluminium. What is the reason for this? Tick **one** box.

☐ Aluminium is unreactive.

☐ Aluminium doesn't react with water and oxygen in the atmosphere.

☐ Aluminium forms an oxide layer on its surface which prevents corrosion.

[1]

2.3 Many ships are made from iron or its alloys. Magnesium blocks can be attached to a ship's hull to prevent corrosion. These react with the air and water around the hull instead of the iron.

Give the name of this process.

....

[1]

[Total 3 marks]

Exam Practice Tip

You might be asked to draw conclusions about corrosion from data that you're given. Remember that when a piece of metal corrodes, it bonds with oxygen and water molecules in the air. This means its mass will always increase.

Topic 10 — Using Resources

Finite and Renewable Resources

1 This question is about sustainable use of the Earth's resources. **Grade 4-5**
   Table 1 shows the time it takes to form various materials.

Table 1

Material	Time to form (years)
Wood	2-20
Coal	3×10^8
Cotton	0.5

1.1 Using the data in **Table 1**, state **one** finite resource. Explain your answer.

   Resource: ....

   Reason: ....
   [2]

1.2 What is meant by the term 'renewable resource'?

   ....
   [1]

1.3 Name **one** other renewable resource that is not listed in **Table 1**.

   ....
   [1]
   [Total 4 marks]

2 Humans have developed items made from both natural and synthetic materials. **Grade 4-5**

2.1 Give **one** example of how agriculture is used to increase the supply of a natural resource.

   ....

   ....
   [1]

2.2 Give **one** example of a synthetic product which has replaced
    or is used in addition to a natural resource.

   ....
   [1]
   [Total 2 marks]

Exam Practice Tip

If numbers are really big or small, they could be given in standard form, like the time taken for coal to form in Table 1 (3×10^8). You can tell how big the number is by looking at the little number next to the 10. If the little number is positive, then the whole number is greater than 1. The higher this little number is, the bigger the whole number will be. If the little number is negative, it means the whole number is between 0 and 1. The more negative this little number is, the smaller the whole number will be. Give this a read a few times until it makes sense.

Topic 10 — Using Resources

Reuse and Recycling

1 Some materials can be recycled into new products.

1.1 Which of the following statements about the recycling of metals is **false**? Tick **one** box.

Recycling metals reduces the amount of waste sent to landfill. ☐

Recycling metals increases the finite amount of metals in the Earth. ☐

Recycling metals often uses less energy than making new metals. ☐

Recycling metals saves some of the finite amount of metals in the Earth. ☐

[1]

1.2 Glass can be recycled and made into new products.
Using the words in the box, complete the sentences below.

| melted | reshaped | less | crushed | more |

Glass products are .... and then ....

They are then .... to make other products for a different use.

This process uses .... energy than making new glass.

[4]

[Total 5 marks]

2 Cups and mugs for hot drinks can be made from different materials.
Two possible materials are stainless steel and paper.
Table 1 gives some information about these materials.

Table 1

	Stainless Steel Mug	**Paper Cup**
Source of raw material	Metal ores and coal	Plant fibre
Can it be reused or recycled?	Both	Possible but not widely done.

2.1 Using the information in **Table 1**, state which of the two raw materials is more sustainable.
Give a reason for your answer.

Raw material: ....

Reason: ....

[2]

2.2 The stainless steel mug can be reused many times.
Suggest why this may make it more sustainable than the paper cup.

....

....

[1]

[Total 3 marks]

Topic 10 — Using Resources

Life Cycle Assessments

Warm-Up

Draw one line between each stage of a product's life and the correct example of that stage.

Life cycle stage	Example
Getting the Raw Materials	Coal being mined from the ground.
Manufacturing and Packaging	Plastic bags going to landfill.
Using the Product	A car using fuel while driving.
Product Disposal	Books being made from wood pulp.

1 What is the purpose of a life cycle assessment? Tick **one** box.

It looks at how many different chemicals are used during the life cycle of a product. ☐

It looks at the total amount of greenhouse gases produced during the life cycle of a product. ☐

It looks at every stage of a product's life to assess the impact on the environment. ☐

It looks at the total economic impact of each stage of a product's life. ☐

[Total 1 mark]

2 A mobile phone company is carrying out a life cycle assessment for one of their products.

2.1 Suggest **one** environmental problem associated with using metals as a raw material.

....
[1]

2.2 The mobile phone is powered by a battery which needs to be recharged regularly. Most electricity comes from burning fossil fuels. Suggest **one** environmental problem that this may cause.

....
[1]

2.3 Mobile phones can be recycled. However, some still get sent to landfill.
Give **two** disadvantages of disposing of rubbish in landfill.

1 ....

2 ....
[2]
[Total 4 marks]

Topic 10 — Using Resources

Using Life Cycle Assessments

1 A company carries out a life cycle assessment (LCA) for a new product. The LCA only shows some of the environmental impacts that are caused by the product. How can this type of LCA be described? Tick **one** box.

limited life cycle assessment ☐

selective life cycle assessment ☐

incomplete life cycle assessment ☐

exclusive life cycle assessment ☐

[Total 1 mark]

2 A new shop is deciding whether to stock plastic bags or paper bags for their customers' shopping. To help them decide, they carry out a life cycle assessment for each type of bag. Some information about each bag is shown in **Table 1**.

Table 1

	Plastic bag	Paper bag
Raw materials	Crude oil	Wood
Manufacture	A little waste produced.	Lots of waste produced.
Using the product	Can be reused several times.	Usually only used once.
Disposal	Recyclable Not biodegradable	Recyclable Biodegradable

2.1 Using the information in **Table 1**, give **two** advantages of plastic bags over paper bags.

1 ....

2 ....

[2]

2.2 Suggest **two** other pieces of information, that are not given in **Table 1**, that would be needed to help decide which bag has the least impact on the environment.

1 ....

2 ....

[2]

[Total 4 marks]

Topic 10 — Using Resources

Potable Water

Warm-Up

Circle the words below which are sources of fresh water.

sewage   reservoirs   oceans   lakes   rivers   underground rocks   seas

---

1 This question is about potable water.

1.1 Which of the following is a correct description of potable water? Tick **one** box.

Pure water ☐

Water with a pH between 4.5 and 6.5 ☐

Water that is safe to drink ☐

Water with a high concentration of salt ☐

[1]

1.2 In the warmer areas of the UK, surface water can dry up. Suggest a suitable source of fresh water that could be used instead for the production of potable water.

....

[1]

[Total 2 marks]

2 Fresh water needs to be treated before it is safe to drink.

2.1 Draw **one** line between each treatment of water and the substances removed by the process.

Passing water through filter beds		Solid Waste
		Microbes
Sterilisation		Chemicals

[2]

2.2 Name **three** things that can be used to sterilise fresh water.

1 ....

2 ....

3 ....

[3]

[Total 5 marks]

Topic 10 — Using Resources

Desalination

1 **Figure 1** shows a set of equipment that could be used to desalinate sea water through a process known as distillation.

Figure 1

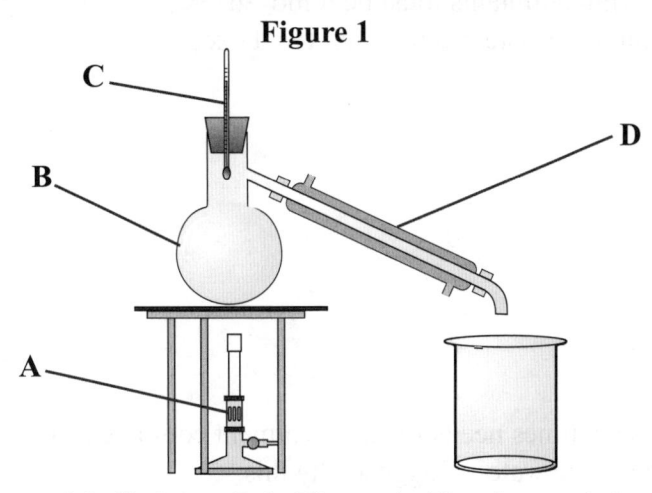

Name the components labelled **A** to **D** in **Figure 1**. Use the words in the box.

| round bottomed flask | condenser | thermometer | Bunsen burner |

A .... B ....

C .... D ....

[Total 4 marks]

2 Before seawater can be used for drinking water, it needs to go through desalination. Desalination is the process of removing salts.

2.1 Reverse osmosis is a type of desalination that uses membranes. Which of the following statements describes how membranes help to purify seawater? Tick **one** box.

The membranes let salt molecules pass through but stop the water from passing. ☐

The membranes let water molecules pass through but trap the salts. ☐

The salt molecules stick to the membranes which are then removed from the water. ☐

The membranes heat the water causing it to evaporate. ☐

[1]

2.2 Although it is surrounded by the sea, the UK produces potable water from fresh water sources, rather than from sea water. Explain why the UK chooses to use fresh water sources.

....

....

[2]

[Total 3 marks]

Exam Practice Tip

Some water costs a lot to make potable, some not so much. Make sure you understand the different processes that salty water and fresh water undergo to make it safe to drink and why the different processes are used in different places.

Topic 10 — Using Resources

Waste Water Treatment

1 Waste water must be treated before being reused or released into the environment.

1.1 Which **two** of the following pollutants must be removed from sewage and agricultural waste water? Tick **two** boxes.

Calcium ions, Ca^{2+} ☐

Organic matter ☐

Harmful microbes ☐

Sodium ions, Na^+ ☐

[2]

1.2 Industrial waste water sometimes needs further treatment compared to sewage and agricultural waste water. Suggest why this.

....
[1]

[Total 3 marks]

2 This question is about the treatment of waste water in the form of sewage.
Figure 1 shows the different stages water goes through at a sewage treatment facility.

Figure 1

Waste Water → Screening → Sedimentation →
- B → aerobic digestion → released into rivers
- A → X → natural gas / fertiliser

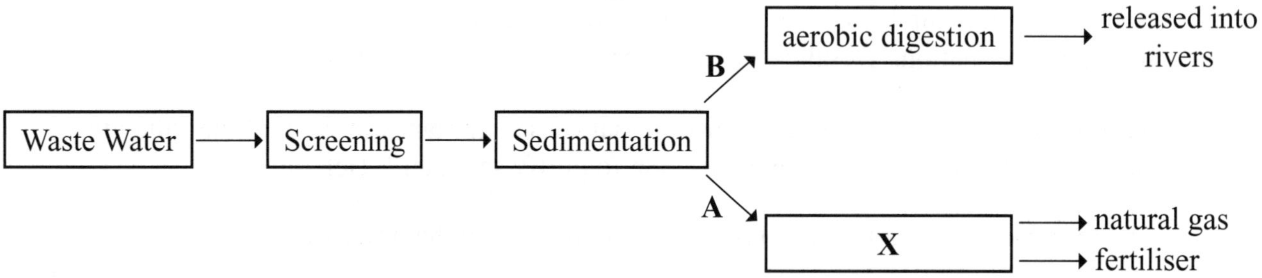

2.1 What is the purpose of the stage described as 'screening'?

....

....
[2]

2.2 What are the names given to the two substances produced by sedimentation?

Substance **A**: ....

Substance **B**: ....

[2]

2.3 What is the name of process **X**?

....
[1]

[Total 5 marks]

Topic 10 — Using Resources

The Haber Process

1 The Haber process is an important chemical process. *(Grade 4-5)*

1.1 Which of these substances is a reactant in the Haber process found in air?
Tick **one** box.

☐ Carbon   ☐ Hydrogen   ☐ Ammonia   ☐ Oxygen   ☐ Nitrogen

[1]

1.2 What is the product of the Haber process?

....
[1]

1.3 Why is the Haber process important to agriculture?

....
[1]

[Total 3 marks]

2 This question is about the Haber process. *(Grade 4-5)*

2.1 Unused reactants from the Haber process are collected and reused.
Why are there always unused reactants from the reaction used in the Haber process?

....

....
[2]

2.2 Explain how the unused reactants are collected and reused.

....

....

....
[3]

2.3 State the catalyst used in the Haber process.

....
[1]

2.4 What effect does adding a catalyst have?

....

....
[1]

[Total 7 marks]

Topic 10 — Using Resources

NPK Fertilisers

1 This question is about some of the raw materials that are used in the production of NPK fertilisers. *(Grade 3-4)*

1.1 Name **two** compounds of potassium that are used to make NPK fertilisers.

1. ....

2. ....
[2]

1.2 How are these compounds obtained from natural deposits in the Earth?

....
[1]
[Total 3 marks]

2 This question is about the chemical processing of phosphate rock that is part of the production of NPK fertilisers. **Figure 1** shows one of the stages involved in the process used to convert phosphate rock into chemicals that are present in NPK fertilisers. *(Grade 4-5)*

Figure 1

Phosphate rock —Nitric acid→ Phosphoric acid + Substance **A**

2.1 Name substance **A**.

....
[1]

2.2 Phosphate rock can also be reacted with sulfuric acid and phosphoric acid. Draw lines to match each pair of reactants to the correct product(s) formed.

phosphate rock + sulfuric acid

phosphate rock + phosphoric acid

calcium phosphate only

calcium phosphate and calcium sulfate

calcium sulfate only
[2]

2.3 The reactions of phosphate rock to produce fertilisers are carried out differently in industry to in the lab. **Table 1** shows how the soluble products are separated from solution in each environment.

Table 1

In the lab	In industry
Crystallisation	Heat is used to evaporate water off

Suggest why crystallisation is not used to separate the reaction products in industry.

....
[1]
[Total 4 marks]

Topic 10 — Using Resources

Mixed Questions

1 **Figure 1** shows the nuclear symbol of a Group 1 element.

Figure 1

$${}^{7}_{3}\text{Li}$$

1.1 Write the name of the element that the symbol in **Figure 1** represents.

....
[1]

1.2 Name another element in the same group as the element shown in **Figure 1**.

....
[1]

1.3 Atoms contain protons, neutrons and electrons. Draw **one** line from each of these particles to show how many there are in an atom of the element shown in **Figure 1**.

Particle	Number in one atom of Li
proton	3
electron	4
neutron	3

[1]

1.4 The element in **Figure 1** is a metal. Which of the following diagrams shows the structure of a metal? Tick **one** box.

[1]

1.5 The element in **Figure 1** reacts with water. One of the products of this reaction is a gas. When a lit splint is placed in the gas, a squeaky popping noise is made. What gas was produced? Tick **one** box.

Carbon dioxide ☐   Chlorine ☐   Oxygen ☐   Hydrogen ☐
[1]

1.6 LiOH is also produced in the reaction between the element in **Figure 1** and water. Complete the sentence below. Use a word from the box.

| oxide | hydroxide | carbonate |

When a Group 1 element reacts with water a metal .... is formed.
[1]

[Total 6 marks]

2 Hydrochloric acid and sodium hydroxide react in a neutralisation reaction.

2.1 A student carries out a titration to find the volume of hydrochloric acid needed to neutralise 25 cm³ of sodium hydroxide. She does the titration three times. Her results are in **Table 1**.

Complete **Table 1** to show the mean volume of hydrochloric acid needed.

Table 1

Repeat	1	2	3	mean
Volume (cm³)	35.65	35.70	35.75	....

[2]

2.2 Calculate the uncertainty of the mean.
Use the equation: uncertainty = range ÷ 2

Uncertainty = ... cm³
[2]

2.3 Phenolphthalein is a narrow-range indicator and universal indicator is a broad-range indicator. Which indicator would be more suitable for carrying out the student's titration? Tick **one** box.

Phenolphthalein ☐   Universal indicator ☐
[1]

2.4 The products of the reaction between hydrochloric acid and sodium hydroxide are sodium chloride and water. Complete the equation below to show this reaction.

.... + NaOH → .... + H$_2$O
[2]

2.5 **Figure 2** is a dot and cross diagram showing the formation of sodium chloride. Complete the right-hand side of **Figure 2**. You should add any charges and electrons that are needed.

Figure 2

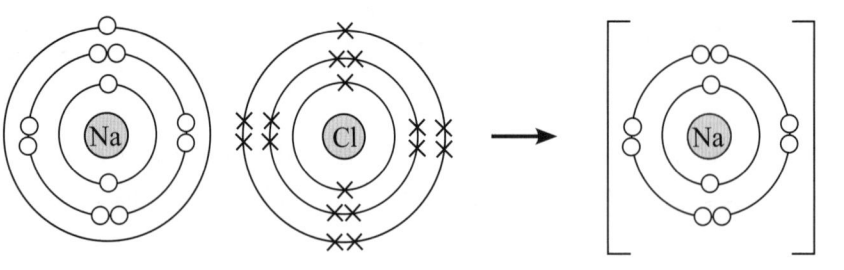

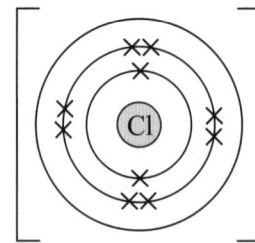

[2]

2.6 State the type of bonding in sodium chloride.

....
[1]

2.7 What colour flame is produced by sodium chloride in a flame test?

....
[1]

[Total 11 marks]

Mixed Questions

3 A substance can be classified as an element, a compound or a mixture. `Grade 3-4`

3.1 Draw a line to connect each type of substance with an example of it.

Type of Substance	Example
compound	salt water
element	nitrogen
mixture	iron oxide

[2]

3.2 Calcium carbonate is a compound with the formula $CaCO_3$.
Name the elements that make up calcium carbonate.

....
[2]

3.3 In terms of the substances they contain, what is the difference between pure water and potable water?

....

....
[2]

3.4 Mixtures can be separated by physical methods.
Name **two** techniques that can be used to separate mixtures

1 ....

2 ....
[2]

[Total 8 marks]

4 Oxygen atoms have the electronic structure 2, 6. `Grade 4-5`

4.1 State which group of the periodic table oxygen is in.
Explain your answer with reference to the electronic structure of oxygen.

Group: ....

Explanation: ....
[2]

4.2 Oxygen can react to form oxide ions. Predict the charge on an oxide ion.
Give a reason for your answer.

Charge: ....

Reason: ....
[2]

4.3 When magnesium reacts with oxygen, it forms magnesium oxide.
What happens to the magnesium? Tick **one** box.

Displacement ☐   Oxidation ☐   Electrolysis ☐   Reduction ☐
[1]

[Total 5 marks]

Mixed Questions

5   Alkanes are hydrocarbon compounds found in crude oil. **Table 2** shows how the boiling points of some alkanes change as the molecules get bigger.

Grade 4-5

Table 2

Alkane	Propane	Butane	Pentane	Hexane	Heptane
Molecular formula	C_3H_8	C_4H_{10}	C_5H_{12}	C_6H_{14}	C_7H_{16}
Boiling point (°C)	−42	−0.5		69	98

5.1 Using the data in **Table 1**, plot a graph of the number of carbon atoms in an alkane molecule against boiling point on the axes below. Draw a smooth curve through the points that you plot.

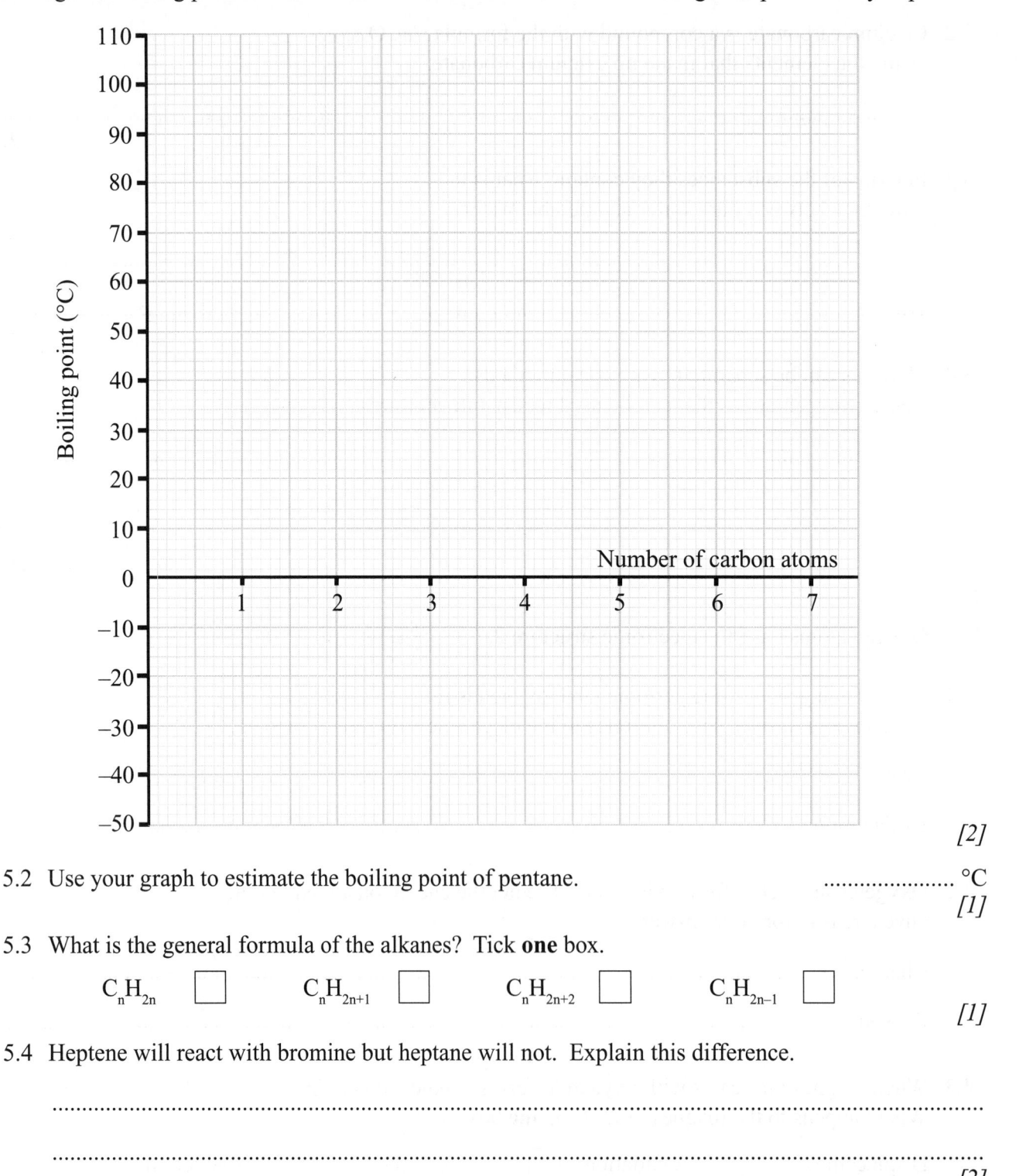

[2]

5.2 Use your graph to estimate the boiling point of pentane. .... °C

[1]

5.3 What is the general formula of the alkanes? Tick **one** box.

C_nH_{2n} ☐ C_nH_{2n+1} ☐ C_nH_{2n+2} ☐ C_nH_{2n-1} ☐

[1]

5.4 Heptene will react with bromine but heptane will not. Explain this difference.

....

....

[2]

[Total 6 marks]

Mixed Questions

6 Chlorine is a Group 7 element that exists as molecules of Cl₂.

6.1 Complete the dot-and-cross diagram below to show the bonding in Cl₂.
You only need to show the outer electron shells.

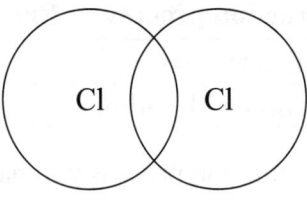

[2]

6.2 Chlorine has two main isotopes — ³⁵Cl and ³⁷Cl. Explain the term 'isotope'.

....

....
[2]

6.3 Describe a test you could carry out for chlorine.
Include any observations you would expect to make.

....

....
[2]

6.4 Predict what happens if you mix chlorine water and sodium iodide solution. Explain your answer.

....

....
[2]
[Total 8 marks]

7 When sodium hydrogen carbonate reacts with ethanoic acid, the temperature of the surroundings decreases.

7.1 Is this reaction endothermic or exothermic?

....
[1]

7.2 Will the energy of the products be higher or lower than the energy of the reactants?

....
[1]

7.3 What effect will increasing the concentration of ethanoic acid have on the rate of the reaction?
Give a reason for your answer.

Effect: ....

Reason: ....

....
[3]
[Total 5 marks]

Mixed Questions

8 Aluminium and iron can be obtained by extracting them from their ores.
Both metals can also be obtained from recycling aluminium and iron items.

Table 3

Material	Extraction process	Energy saved by recycling
Aluminium	Electrolysis	Around 95%
Iron	Reduction with carbon	Around 60%

8.1 Look at **Table 3**. Suggest which extraction process will have a larger carbon footprint.
Give a reason for your answer.

Extraction process: ....

Reason: ....

....

....
[4]

8.2 **Table 3** shows that energy is saved when aluminium and iron are obtained from recycled metals rather than being extracted from their ores. Give **two** other advantages of recycling metals.

1 ....

2 ....
[2]
[Total 6 marks]

9 A student has two salt solutions, **A** and **B**. Solution **A** is blue but solution **B** is colourless.
One of these solutions contains a transition metal salt.

9.1 Suggest which solution contains a transition metal salt.

....
[1]

9.2 Explain your answer.

....
[1]

9.3 One of the salt solutions contains potassium.
Outline how the student could carry out a flame test to show that the salt contains potassium.
Your answer should include the result the student should expect to observe.

....

....

....

....
[4]
[Total 6 marks]

Mixed Questions

10 Methyl ethanoate and water are formed when methanol and ethanoic acid react.

10.1 What type of organic compound is methyl ethanoate?

....

[1]

10.2 The equation for this reaction is: $CH_3OH + CH_3COOH \rightarrow CH_3OOCCH_3 + H_2O$
Calculate the relative formula mass (M_r) of methanol and ethanoic acid.
Atomic masses (A_r): H = 1, C = 12, O = 16.

M_r of methanol = ...

M_r of ethanoic acid = ...

[2]

10.3 A student attempts to make methyl ethanoate using the reaction above.
Calculate the atom economy of this reaction. Give your answer to 2 significant figures.
The relative formula mass of methyl ethanoate is 74.

Atom economy = ... %

[3]

[Total 6 marks]

11* The structure and bonding of substances affects their properties.

Table 4

	Hardness	Melting point	Conducts electricity?
Diamond	Hard	High	No
Graphite	Soft	High	Yes

Explain how the structure and bonding of diamond and graphite give them the properties listed in **Table 4**.

Your answer should include details of how the atoms are arranged and how they're held together.

....

....

....

....

....

....

....

[Total 6 marks]

Mixed Questions

The Periodic Table

	Group 1	Group 2											Group 3	Group 4	Group 5	Group 6	Group 7	Group 0
1							1 H Hydrogen 1											4 He Helium 2
2	7 Li Lithium 3	9 Be Beryllium 4											11 B Boron 5	12 C Carbon 6	14 N Nitrogen 7	16 O Oxygen 8	19 F Fluorine 9	20 Ne Neon 10
3	23 Na Sodium 11	24 Mg Magnesium 12											27 Al Aluminium 13	28 Si Silicon 14	31 P Phosphorus 15	32 S Sulfur 16	35.5 Cl Chlorine 17	40 Ar Argon 18
4	39 K Potassium 19	40 Ca Calcium 20	45 Sc Scandium 21	48 Ti Titanium 22	51 V Vanadium 23	52 Cr Chromium 24	55 Mn Manganese 25	56 Fe Iron 26	59 Co Cobalt 27	59 Ni Nickel 28	63.5 Cu Copper 29	65 Zn Zinc 30	70 Ga Gallium 31	73 Ge Germanium 32	75 As Arsenic 33	79 Se Selenium 34	80 Br Bromine 35	84 Kr Krypton 36
5	85 Rb Rubidium 37	88 Sr Strontium 38	89 Y Yttrium 39	91 Zr Zirconium 40	93 Nb Niobium 41	96 Mo Molybdenum 42	98 Tc Technetium 43	101 Ru Ruthenium 44	103 Rh Rhodium 45	106 Pd Palladium 46	108 Ag Silver 47	112 Cd Cadmium 48	115 In Indium 49	119 Sn Tin 50	122 Sb Antimony 51	128 Te Tellurium 52	127 I Iodine 53	131 Xe Xenon 54
6	133 Cs Caesium 55	137 Ba Barium 56	139 La Lanthanum 57	178 Hf Hafnium 72	181 Ta Tantalum 73	184 W Tungsten 74	186 Re Rhenium 75	190 Os Osmium 76	192 Ir Iridium 77	195 Pt Platinum 78	197 Au Gold 79	201 Hg Mercury 80	204 Tl Thallium 81	207 Pb Lead 82	209 Bi Bismuth 83	[209] Po Polonium 84	[210] At Astatine 85	[222] Rn Radon 86
7	[223] Fr Francium 87	[226] Ra Radium 88	[227] Ac Actinium 89	[261] Rf Rutherfordium 104	[262] Db Dubnium 105	[266] Sg Seaborgium 106	[264] Bh Bohrium 107	[277] Hs Hassium 108	[268] Mt Meitnerium 109	[271] Ds Darmstadtium 110	[272] Rg Roentgenium 111	[285] Cn Copernicium 112	[286] Uut Ununtrium 113	[289] Fl Flerovium 114	[289] Uup Ununpentium 115	[293] Lv Livermorium 116	[294] Uus Ununseptium 117	[294] Uuo Ununoctium 118

Relative atomic mass
Atomic (proton) number

The Lanthanides (atomic numbers 58-71) and the Actinides (atomic numbers 90-103) are not shown in this table.